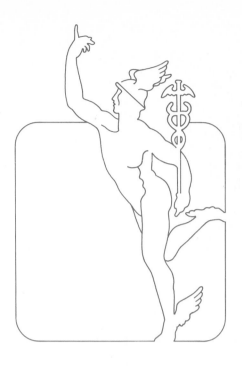

WORLD OF CULTURE

MYTHOLOGY

by

David Leeming

Pictorial Narrative by

Edwin Bayrd

Newsweek Books, New York

NEWSWEEK BOOKS

Joseph L. Gardner, Editor

Janet Czarnetzki, Art Director
Edwin Bayrd, Associate Editor
Laurie Platt Winfrey, Picture Editor
Kathleen Berger, Copy Editor

S. Arthur Dembner, President
Alvin Garfin, Publisher

ARNOLDO MONDADORI EDITORE

Mariella De Battisti, Picture Researcher
Giovanni Adamoli, Production Coordinator

Frontispiece: The Hindu god of creation, Vishnu, and his wife, astride a fantastic bird

Grateful acknowledgment is made for the use of excerpted material from the following works:
Enûma elish. Reprinted from *The Babylonian Genesis* by Alexander Heidel by permission of the University of Chicago Press. Copyright © 1942 and 1951 by the University of Chicago.
Hesiod: The Poems and Fragments translated by A.W. Mair. Copyright © 1908 by Oxford University Press. Reprinted by permission of the publisher.
The Homeric Hymns translated by Charles Boer. Copyright © 1970 by the Swallow Press, Chicago.
Kojiki translated by Donald L. Philippi. Copyright © 1968 by University of Tokyo Press. Reprinted by permission of the publisher.
The Lake Isle of Innisfree by William Butler Yeats. Copyright © 1906 by Macmillan Publishing Co., Inc., renewed 1934 by William Butler Yeats. Reprinted by permission of the publisher.
Memories, Dreams, Reflections by C.G. Jung. Recorded and edited by Aniela Jaffe, translated by Richard and Clara Winston. Copyright © 1961, 1962, 1963 by Pantheon Books, a division of Random House, Inc.
The Odyssey by Homer. Translated by Albert Cook. Copyright © 1974 by Norton Critical Editions, New York. Reprinted by permission of the publisher, W.W. Norton.
The Poetic Edda translated by Lee M. Hollander. Copyright © 1928 by University of Texas Press. Reprinted by permission of the translator and publisher.
Popol Vuh: The Sacred Book of the Ancient Quiché Maya from the translation of Adrian Recinos. Copyright © 1950 by University of Oklahoma Press. Reprinted by permission of the publisher.
The Shrines of Tut-Ankh-Amon from *Egyptian Religious Texts and Representations.* Edited by Alexandre Piankoff, Bollingen Series XL, vol. 2. Copyright © 1955 by Bollingen Foundation and reprinted by permission of Princeton University Press.
A Vedic Reader for Students by A.A. Macdonell. Copyright © 1971 by Oxford University Press. Reprinted by permission of the publisher.

Contents

1

Primitive Fears, Universal Understandings

THE WORDS AND IMAGES of mythology express man's sense of what he is in relation to the cosmos. As man's life has changed over the centuries so have the external forms of his myths—but the inner structure of those myths has remained essentially the same. As a result, any given mythic story is a combination of superstition and religious truth, of primitive fears and universal understandings. This being the case, it is illogical if not impossible to approach mythology from a single point of view. Instead, this elusive yet intriguing subject must be explored from several different viewpoints, from divergent perspectives that will provide us with a comprehensive composite portrait.

The first chapter of this book will consider mythology from the cultural perspective, proffering a historical survey of several of the more important ethnic mythologies. Next we will explore the meaning of myths, particularly myths that seek to explain complex scientific phenomena or obscure historical facts. It will then be possible to consider ways in which myths transcend history and culture to reveal common human emotions and the collective dreams of the human race. A separate chapter will explore those dreams in detail, suggesting how the hero took shape from them. The mythmaking process, primarily as it is revealed in poetry and folk literature, will be the subject of yet another section, one in which it will be seen that the mythmaker himself can best be understood as a mythic hero. The final chapter will relate mythology to life in the second half of the twentieth century.

The story of mythology begins sometime in the distant reaches of prehistory, when man first awakened to a consciousness of his existence. The life of prehistoric man was a brutal battle against extinction, and for thousands of years it was necessary to kill constantly in order to eat and avoid being eaten. It is hardly surprising, then, that such Paleolithic art as exists—primarily rough figurines and cave paintings—indicates the rudiments of a mythology dominated by the essential tasks involved in the survival of the race. The images are of hunting, of men clad in animal skins, antlers, and masks participating in hunting rituals, and of women—apparently fertility goddesses—with exaggerated sexual characteristics.

The nature of the mythologies that produced this art is largely a matter of conjecture. As he looked about him, primitive man must have noticed certain patterns in his surroundings. The sun, which produced

Gross and enigmatic, the unlovely figurine opposite is a mother goddess, or so-called Venus figure, from Catal Huyuk, a sixth millennium B.C. Neolithic site in what is now Turkey. A primitive fertility figure, she represents man's earliest mythmaking impulses.

both light and warmth, moved regularly across the open sky. Its arrival and departure were generally marked by great blazes of color. During the periods when the sun was gone, an even more mysterious object appeared in the sky, providing a small amount of light in darkness. And this object, the moon, changed size over a period of time. Primitive man must also have noticed that during periods of sustained cold, plants withered up—and that during periods of warmth they proliferated.

The coming of darkness and the onset of winter must have frightened prehistoric man, and such phenomena as eclipses and thunderstorms must have been terrifying in the extreme. It seems logical to assume, under the circumstances, that primitive humans would have attempted to ensure the regular return of the sun, the moon, and green plants. Noting that the sun and moon both moved, prehistoric man probably assumed that they were alive and somehow conscious. If this were so, it might be possible to convince them to do what man wanted them to do. Perhaps through imitation, early man reasoned, these "other beings" could be persuaded to comply—and he proceeded to develop dance rituals with costumes to that end. One can imagine the mysterious moon being played by women and the sun by men. (Paleolithic paintings and figurines suggest a dominance of women and moon-mother goddess cults in the religions of the times.) The importance of the female element in early mythology is almost certainly the result of primitive man's awareness of his dependence on reproduction for survival—and his inability to perceive that the male had any function in reproduction. As to the connection between the female and the moon, this can be directly attributed to the moon's phases, which were inevitably associated with the twenty-eight days of the menstrual cycle and which were, probably from a very early date, also associated with the changing of girth caused by pregnancy. Stories would naturally have developed concerning this sky mother. One suggested that she returned to the earth during the day—and thus was an earth mother too. Another claimed that she produced offspring in the form of edible plants, and was therefore a provider.

The sun, meanwhile, with its blaze of light and color, emerged as a male god—a lover and hunter—and when the connection between coitus and childbirth was finally made, the sun became a significant mythological figure as a fertility initiator. During the period in which the female of the species dominated religion, a period extending well into Neolithic times, the moon was represented on earth by a moon queen and the sun by a sun king who, in his distinctly subservient role, was frequently used as a sacrificial victim. When the power of the sun died at midwinter it was thought necessary to sacrifice the sun king in order to restore warmth to the planet. A complicated cult of the sacred king developed from this practice—a cult, well rooted in northern Europe, that extended into Africa and across the sea to Central America. In time, of course, skeptical (or merely prudent) monarchs began to have second thoughts about being sacrificed to the Great Mother, and in this period several cultures simultaneously developed the practice of "permitting" an honored subject to make the dark journey in the king's stead. As the goddess seemed to accept the substitution,

mythic traditions arose in virtually every civilization, traditions in which a great hero took upon himself the burden of death and traveled to the underworld for the good of his people.

The next step in the development of mythology occurred sometime between the seventh and fourth millenniums B.C. By that time the moon-earth mother religion had become firmly connected with the art of soil cultivation. Hunting was being widely supplemented by the art of animal husbandry, which was rapidly taking the place of the nomad's ceaseless search for meat. When these two arts—the cultivation of the soil and the domestication of animals—met somewhere in the Neolithic world, the inevitable result was the establishment of a pattern of stationary village life and, eventually, urban culture. This in turn permitted the development of the religious systems that we associate with particular races or societies—the systems that have evolved into the great world mythologies.

At archaeological sites in the Near East, objects have been found that we now recognize as symbols of man's mythologies. In Samarra, a site on the Tigris River, images shaped like the Maltese cross and swastika have been uncovered indicating that these symbols originated long before the world knew of Christ or Hitler. And south of the Taurus range (the Bull Mountains of southern Turkey) archaeologists have found instances in which images of a bull, a goddess, and a double ax have been placed together in obvious replication of a sacrifice ritual. Similar combinations occur later in such places as Persia, Crete, and Mexico, where bulls were commonly sacrificed to the Great Mother. The area in which these discoveries have occurred extends from Asia Minor to the Persian Gulf and is bounded by the Tigris and Euphrates rivers. The region is known as Mesopotamia or Babylon. The mythologies that arose in this extraordinarily mythogenetic (or "myth-bearing") zone have, in turn, given rise to much of Western tradition.

The mystery of maternity—a central tenet in man's earliest mythologies—is represented in mother-child images from Cyprus (left, above), India (left, below), Mycenaean Greece (above), and pre-Columbian America (below).

Mesopotamia itself was occupied as early as 4000 B.C. by a mysterious race of non-Semitic people whom we call the Sumerians and whose original home and linguistic roots are unknown. Among their other achievements, the Sumerians invented a form of writing that was eventually adopted, with modification, in many parts of the Near East. It is to a great extent because of this writing and the record it provides that scholars often say history begins at Sumer. This method of writing, called cuneiform, reveals the Sumerians as an intelligent, agricultural, animal-raising people—inhabitors of several important cities and possessors of a rich mythology. This mythology was, with relatively few modifications, adopted by the ancient peoples who successively conquered and occupied Mesopotamia.

The first conquerors of the Tigris-Euphrates basin were a Semitic people who invaded and later colonized the northern part of this fertile region. They spoke Akkadian, a language that would later develop into Arabic, and they founded the great city-state now known as Akkad. King Sargon I, their leader, is the subject of one of the oldest transmitted hero myths—a myth with a familiar ring to it. According to this legend, Sargon was born of a virgin and an unknown father, was placed in a basket of reeds, and was dropped into a river—from which he was

rescued by a passing water carrier. Later Sargon became king and was beloved by the Sumerian-Akkadian Great Mother.

As the Akkadians pressed southward and gradually overcame the Sumerians, they adopted both the cuneiform script and the religion of their predecessors. In fact, the invaders preserved the Sumerian language itself for religious purposes, rather as the Romans preserved Greek and the Christian Europeans Latin.

In time Mesopotamia was to be invaded by a second wave of Semitic people, the biblical Amorites, who established their first dynasty in the city of Babylon. The Amorites, also known as Babylonians, gradually gained control over the Akkadians and the Sumerians and by late in the third millennium B.C. Babylon had enveloped all of Mesopotamia. The Babylonians also took over the ancient cuneiform script and the Sumerian religion.

About 1700 B.C. Babylon was invaded by yet another Semitic people who had originally settled high up in the Tigris valley and who had been ruled by the Babylonians from *c.* 1950 to 1850 B.C. The Assyrians, as these warriors were called, soon conquered the entire valley, establishing a capital at Nineveh and an important city at Assur. The Assyrians, like the Semitic tribes before them, adopted the script and culture of the old Sumerians. By this time, of course, ancient Sumerian mythology had been so altered and colored by the various peoples who had taken it over that it should properly be called Mesopotamian rather than Sumerian. Indeed, the myths themselves have been found on tablets in all parts of the region that was once Mesopotamia, but the most complete versions are on copies commissioned in the seventh century B.C. by King Ashurbanipal for his library at Nineveh.

According to these records the Mesopotamian pantheon was composed of an "assembly of gods," an organization of deities that reflected the organization of the world. Family life was central, and consequently there were fathers, mothers, brothers, and sisters among the immortals. There were also political hierarchies equivalent to those of the city-state governments.

A dominant theme in Mesopotamian mythology was fertility, always connected with a Great Mother goddess, descended from the Paleolithic moon-goddesses of an earlier age. This Great Mother, called Inanna by the Sumerians and Ishtar by the Semitic invaders, represented the earth, love, and fertility. Her mate was Dumuzi or Tammuz, a vegetation god descended from earlier sun-gods. Equally important was the king of the panethon, the sky-god Anu. Like most of the gods of natural phenomena, Anu contained elements of both good and evil.

An exception was Enki or Ea, the water-god, who brought wisdom and civilization to mankind. His opposite was Nergal, the god of disease and death, who ruled in the Land of No Return. Thus, in the case of the Enki-Nergal relationship, the dark and light sides of the immortals were expressed in two personalities rather than in the same being.

Finally, the Mesopotamians had a moon-god, Nanna or Sin, and a sun-god, Uttu or Shamash. And as Mesopotamian religions became increasingly patriarchal, the Great Mothers were relegated to a secondary status vis-à-vis these great sky-gods and their sacred sons. Yet even the creation of a moon-god could not destroy the basic male-female, sun-moon polarity. It is more than merely coincidental, then, that Nanna represented mystery, intuition, and prophecy—qualities that have always been associated with women—while Uttu was associated with such traditionally male attributes as reason and justice.

One of the primary vehicles for Mesopotamian mythology was the great *Epic of Gilgamesh*. In both its fragmented Sumerian form and in later, more complete Babylonian versions, this remarkable work records the feats of a legendary Sumerian king, Gilgamesh, slayer of a dragon-like, fire-breathing giant. This immensely long and extremely discursive narrative follows Gilgamesh as he descends to where he seeks eternal life and where he is told the tale of the Great Flood by a wise old man. All this was recorded before 2000 B.C., making Gilgamesh the first character in all of world literature to perform the ritual acts that have become basic to the adventures of the mythological hero.

The Mesopotamians were not the only neolithic peoples to produce a sophisticated mythology, of course. The Canaanites, Semitic contemporaries of the Mesopotamians, possessed a body of myth that is generally referred to as Ugaritic because of tablets discovered on the site of the ancient city of Ugarit. And elsewhere in Asia Minor distinctive mythologies were evolved by the Hittites, the Hurrians, and the Phrygians (who worshiped one of the greatest of the Great Mothers, Cybele). Nonetheless, after that of the Mesopotamians the most important mythology of the Near East was that of Egypt.

Egypt lay in its own fertile and productive river valley and as a result Egyptian mythology shared with the Mesopotamian a special emphasis on fertility. The central figures in the former fertility cult were the dying maize-god Osiris, his sister-wife Isis, and his evil brother Set. This myth, which is related to that of Dumuzi and Inanna, was closely associated with the life-giving annual flooding of the Nile and with the ritual of mummification in preparation for the ultimate flood, which was death.

After the cult of Osiris, Egypt's dominant myth was that of the god Ra, creator of the world. He was the leader of a pantheon that included many gods, many of whom took at least partial animal form. Anubis, god of the dead, was a jackal. Sebek was a crocodile; Horus was a falcon; and Thoth, god of the moon, was depicted as an ibis or a baboon. Cult centers, presided over by particular gods, were formed all over Egypt. Like the Mesopotamian immortals, each of these tutelary gods had a family. At Memphis, an ancient capital of Lower Egypt, Ptah was the father, lion-headed Sekhmet the mother, and Nefertum, who sported a lotus flower on his head, the son. In the Upper Egyptian city of Thebes, on the other hand, Amon ruled supreme. His consort was Mut, whose name means "mother," and their son was the moon-god Khons. Through his association with the sun-god Ra, Amon soon became the most important of the father gods and was called Amon-Ra.

The sun itself played a significant role in earliest Egyptian mythology, but over the centuries it gradually ceded primacy to other deities. By the eighteenth dynasty (1567–1320 B.C.) worship of Amon–Ra had virtually disappeared. Then the pharaoh Amenhotep IV ascended the Egyptian throne. Under the new name Akhnaton, history's first great monotheist was to abolish the old pantheon by fiat and institute worship of a single deity, the sun-god Aten, who was always represented as a solar disk. Aten was a combination of qualities found in Amon–Ra, Osiris, and the Mesopotamian Enki as well. With Akhnaton's death however, polytheistic religion was revived by Egypt's priestly caste, and the temples to Aten were largely destroyed. What could not be destroyed was the concept of monotheism, which eventually blossomed in the Near East as Judaism, Zoroastrianism, and, later, Christianity and Islam.

In time, much of Mesopotamian and Egyptian mythology filtered north and west through Minoan Crete to ancient Greece, the region which produced the mythology that has most obviously influenced Western culture. (Later the Greek religion would be incorporated by the Romans, becoming what we now call Greco-Roman mythology.) The first thing that comes to mind when we think of Greek mythology is a pantheon headed by Zeus, a bearded god beautifully formed in the classical tradition. Zeus, who dwelled on Mount Olympus, was patriarch of a powerful family, as was Jupiter, Zeus's Roman equivalent.

The manner in which the Greeks approached these gods has its analogue in the way villagers approach the family of the wealthy squire. To their faces, these gods were praised and worshiped; behind their backs, they were made the butts of countless stories that depicted them as spoiled, quarrelsome, stingy, jealous, and lacking concern for the welfare of their vassals, the human race. Zeus was known as a philanderer; his wife, Hera (Juno), as a nagger; their daughter Aphrodite (Venus) as a loose woman; their son Ares (Mars) as a bully. Another daughter of Zeus, Athena (Minerva), was believed to be a difficult if wise spinster. And still another offspring, Hermes (Mercury), a trickster and troublemaker. Yet elements of the old Near Eastern religions were there. Apollo was a sun-god, and his sister Artemis (Diana) was a moon-goddess.

Equally important was the survival—well into Roman times—of popular mystery cults that coexisted with the official religion of the Olympians in all parts of Greece. These cults were the continuation of the old fertility religions; their central personalities were Demeter (Ceres) and the "foreign" god Dionysus (Bacchus). Dionysus was frequently described as a son of Zeus, but his origins are lost in prehistory, and unlike his brothers and sisters on Olympus he was essentially a god of the earth. In his death and return to life Dionysus resembled his Mesopotamian and Egyptian counterparts, Dumuzi and

Osiris; and it was said that while still a small child he had been dis-membered and devoured by the Titans, those evil forces of the inner earth. His phallus was not eaten, however, and from it sprang the resur-rected god himself. Therefore in ancient Dionysian rituals an image of the god's phallus was carried in procession by the priestess of the Great Mother. The primary celebrants of the rituals of Dionysus were women, and we are told that the devotees of the cult would work themselves into a frenzy, chanting and dancing until they could envi-sion in a sacrificial animal the presence of the god. This animal they tore to pieces and ate, thus taking the god into themselves so that they might be renewed by his regenerative power.

The myth of Dionysus remained a central element in Greek mythology even during that culture's golden age. The great dramatic festivals of Periclean Athens were held in honor of Dionysus, in the hopes that he might cause the city to prosper. Scholars have shown that the plays of this period, with their ritual dances and chanting, their sac-rifice of the hero, and their emphasis on final regeneration, developed directly out of ancient ritual. It is not insignificant in this connection that the guests of honor at such festivals were the priests of Dionysus, or that a remnant of the sacrificial altar always remained on stage.

This sacrificial, ritual element can be seen in almost all Greek trage-dies, and it is emphatically evident in the most famous tragedy of them all, *Oedipus Rex*. Oedipus's sin—the killing of his father and the marry-ing of his mother—is so improbable as to indicate a purpose governed by ritual rather than realism. This king is shown to be guilty of the worst of sins so that it will be unmistakably clear to the audience that he is the sacred king—the one who carries the sins of the whole society as a burden, the one who must suffer for the good of all. It is clear, too, that Oedipus does not commit his sins willingly or knowingly; rather, he is chosen by the gods for his ritual role—and therefore blame, in the usual sense, is not involved. Furthermore, the wedding of the young king and the much older queen is in itself indicative of ancient matriar-chal practices—those in which an ageless moon queen is provided with a succession of kings who are sacrificed at regular intervals.

Men have always preferred to think of their gods in human terms, and thus it is hardly surprising that each of the great mythologies we have considered is dominated by a family unit consisting of a father, mother, and a very unusual son. Clearly, then, fertility and procreation have been vitally important to Western man since the beginning of civ-ilization, and as a result man has viewed the cosmos as an extension of the family, organized in the same manner.

This is not to say that the fertility theme has always been treated in the same way. In the Dumuzi-Inanna and Osiris-Isis relationships, for instance, the women in many ways predominate. This is only natural in a strongly matriarchal society, of course, and particularly in one, like the Sumerian or Egyptian, that places particular emphasis on plant fer-tility. Among the Greeks this emphasis on the female was largely subli-mated—in the mystery cults of Demeter and in those of Dionysus and his female attendants. In the official religion it was the male principle that prevailed, and fertility was not an expressed concern. The same was true in both Judaism and Christianity; sexuality was not deemed a virtue and the female principle was often altogether absent. And by the time the New Testament was written woman had become a symbolic rather than an active participant in the great death and resurrection mystery. In her sorrow at Calvary, Mary inevitably reminds us of those other Great Mothers, Inanna and Isis, but her physical presence there is peripheral and symbolic. The fertility of Jesus is spiritual rather than physical; it is not crops that he will bring back from the dead, but souls.

Perhaps the major contribution of the fertility myth to the Western world view is the sense it conveys of redemption through suffering. In each case a god-hero—Dumuzi, Osiris, Dionysus, or Christ—provides an alternative to the "justice" of the father god. Through the hero's suffering—and, often, his death—mankind is shown a way to break out of the tragic cycle of life. Death becomes the path to resurrection and eternal life. And thus when the modern psychiatrist tells us that we must lose ourselves to find ourselves he echoes the implicit message of Enki in his struggles with his dark opposite, Nergal, of Inanna with her sister Ereshkigal, of Osiris with his evil brother Set, of Dionysus with the Titans, and of Job and Jesus with a world infected by Satan. The message of Western mythology is that the quest is agonizing but that the goal, eternal life—the goal sought by that earliest of heroes, Gilgamesh—is well worth the effort.

While it is true that the mythologies of Mesopotamia, Egypt, and Greece have been the most influential upon our own culture, it would be misleading to ignore the other significant mythological systems produced by man in his search for the meaning of his existence in the cosmos. Yet to properly survey the mythologies of the world we would have to examine the legends and religions of each of the world's ethnic groups—and in many cases we would have to break each of those ethnic groups into tribes. We would have to study the complex and distinctive mythologies of countless African tribes and those of the great civilizations of the Americas—and even then we would have but scratched the surface. There would still be the myths of the Eskimos, the Celts, and the Persians—and the far more elaborate cosmologies of the Orient, particularly China and Japan.

Much of the essence of these disparate mythologies will be conveyed by the many stories contained in the ensuing chapters of this book. There are, however, two mythogenetic zones that we have not yet considered, regions possessing mythologies of such importance that it is necessary to review them briefly here. These are the mythologies of India and of Northern Europe.

No civilization is more steeped in mythology than that of the Indian subcontinent. India is a land of many gods, some of whom take many forms, but at the same time, Indian mythology is monotheistic, in the sense that everything that exists stems from and is an expression of an absolute to which the name Brahman is given. Brahman is by nature and definition ineffable. "All that exists is Brahman," says the ancient scripture. "Brahman is truth; the world is illusion."

India's oldest extant religious work is the *Rig Veda*, a collection of hymns composed around 1300 B.C. in a form of Sanskrit. (Its authors

were the Aryans, who had settled in India some five hundred years earlier.) The primary figure in the Vedic pantheon of gods is Indra. This remarkable god was said to have been born from his mother's side—and after drinking a magical brew he grew to such enormous size as to cause his father, the sky, and his mother, the earth, to separate forever. Indra became the champion of the Adityas, gentle beings who existed before our universe was created. He led them to victory against the evil Danavas, out of the stomach of whose chief, Vrita, came the female cosmic waters. These waters, who named Indra their lord, were the basis for the establishment of order in the universe.

Toward the end of the Vedic period Indra's dominant role was challenged by those who named a new deity, Prajapati(Brahma), "Lord of Creation." Prajapati is more an abstraction than an anthropomorphic being, and he represents a major step in the direction of Brahmanic philosophizing in Indian mythology—a tendency that parallels the tendency to produce gods with particular personalities. This latter trait is embodied in the dominant gods of modern Hinduism, Vishnu and Shiva. These gods are syncretic; which is to say that they contain in themselves many separate gods. This is especially true of Vishnu, who is at once the conqueror Vikrama, the sun Surya, and several other avatars who to this day are worshiped separately in shrines all over India. Of the many avatars of Vishnu, ten are major. The best known of these are Rama Chandra, Krishna, and the historical Gautama Buddha.

The story of Rama Chandra, the seventh avatar, is told in the *Ramayana*. According to this Sanskrit epic it was Rama who brought the Brahmanic or Aryan culture to southern India. After defeating an evil power called Ravana, Rama Chandra was to rule for 10,000 years over a kingdom in which there was no death, disease, or crime. At the end of this period Rama returned to his ultimate form as Vishnu and led his people directly to heaven, bypassing death.

The eighth avatar, Krishna, is found in the *Bhagavata Purana* of the eighth century A.D. and in the older *Vishnu Purana*. In both he is a pastoral hero, and only in an ancient epic, the *Mahabharata*, is he described as a warrior. In the latter form he worships Shiva and befriends Arjuna, the general of the righteous Pandavas, who are at war with the evil Kauravas. The best known section of the *Mahabharata* is the *Bhagavad Gita*, or "Song of the Blessed One," in which Krishna counsels Arjuna concerning killing when it is done in the name of righteousness.

According to Hindu mythology, the ninth avatar of Vishnu was Gautama Buddha, an actual historical figure who lived in northeast India between about 563 and 483 B.C. Out of Gautama's teachings grew what was to become a new religion, Buddhism, that ultimately won more converts in other parts of Asia than in India. Legend now holds that the Buddha had already experienced many incarnations before he was conceived miraculously by Queen Mahamaya, who in a dream saw a bodhisattva enter her womb in the form of a beautiful white elephant. The birth itself was remarkable, for the Buddha was born without the usual pain, blood, and waters of childbirth. The boy, named Siddhartha, would later forsake the security of home and kingship for higher truths, and he would preach his message to all who would listen.

The other great syncretic Indian god, Shiva, probably originated in the Harappa culture of the Indus valley as early as the third millennium B.C. He is associated with serpents and is called Pashupati, or "Lord of Creatures," in one of his aspects, but like Vishnu he has many forms. He is a god of storms; he is Rudra, the righteous avenger; and he is the god most associated with yoga and meditative asceticism. Perhaps most important, Shiva is the lord of the cosmic dance of creation—life, death, and regeneration.

Shiva's wife, Parvati, is also a creation of Harappa civilization. As a Great Mother she is an Eastern equivalent of Inanna, Isis, Demeter, and Cybele. Her cult has never been totally accepted by Brahmanical Hinduism, but Parvati is worshiped in various forms in many sections of India. Sometimes she is called Ambika, the slayer of demons. Sometimes she is Kali, who danced so furiously as to frighten the gods themselves. And sometimes she is a many-armed goddess who rides upon a lion and demands sacrifices. Finally, the most important, Parvati represents the feminine principle that many Hindus consider the dominant force in the universe. This feminine principle, Shakti, is seen as necessary in all gods. As a religious ode in the *Saundaryalahari* says, "If Shiva is united with Shakti, he is able to exert his power as lord; if not, the god is not able to stir."

Archaeological evidence indicates that the Great Mother cult—of which the Shakti, or tantric, cults were a part—was the earliest in India, just as the matriarchal cults were antecedent to the patriarchal mythologies of Mesopotamia, Egypt, and Greece. It should be noted that even when this matriarchal element has been suppressed by an official patriarchal religion it has nevertheless emerged because of the natural human instinct toward a balanced view of existence, whether that be expressed by the union of *yin* and *yang* in Chinese mythology, by the assumption of the Virgin Mary in Christianity, or by the marriage of Shiva and Parvati in India.

Far to the northwest of India, in what we now call Northern Europe, a wholly separate mythology was to develop in prehistoric times. In the early Christian era this collection of tales was finally set down in a series of anonymous poems called the Eddas, followed in

Shiva, second of the two great syncretic Hindu gods, appears in the ninth-century bronze opposite, above, with his wife, Parvati, yet another in the long line of mother goddesses. Below, Krishna, the eighth avatar of Vishnu, is caught in a dancing pose by an eighteenth-century Nepalese artist. The same god is the warrior-hero of the Mahabharata; that epic's central event—the battle of Kurukshetra—is a confrontation between good and evil (fabric detail at right).

about 1220 by the *Prose Edda*, the work of an Icelandic scholar, Snorri Sturluson. This mythology was primarily Germanic in origin, but the stories themselves originated in Iceland, Germany, and Scandinavia.

In Northern European mythology the center of the universe was the world tree, the great Ash Yggdrasill, the branches of which spread out over heaven and earth. This tree's three roots stretched, respectively, to the land of the gods, to the land of the frost giants, and to the land of the dead. Beneath the roots were various sacred waters and at its base lay a great serpent. The land of the gods was called Asgard and was presided over by Odin, called the "All Father" because he had created the world of humans. He was also called the "One-Eyed" because he had given up an eye in order to drink at the sacred spring of wisdom under Yggdrasill. Above all, Odin was the god of the mysteries and magic; he was a master shaman, and in keeping with that role he was the patron of prophecy and of poetry.

The other gods of the northern pantheon were known collectively as the Aesir. The most important of their number was Thor, son of Odin. He was a warrior-god and, specifically, a killer of the much-feared giants who constantly threatened the Aesir and the world in general. This god of thunder and lightning was known for his magic belt, his iron gloves, and his great hammer, Mjollnir. The ancient Scandinavians believed that thunder sounded when Thor's chariot crossed the heavens, and that lightning struck whenever the god threw his hammer to the ground.

A more pleasant son of Odin was the beautiful and much-loved Balder. Snorri says of him, "He is so handsome in his appearance and so brilliant that he gives off light, and he carries a white wildflower with which his own fair lashes have been compared." Balder lived in a kind of Eden in the sky. Significantly, it was to this gentle and beloved god that tragedy was to come. After a series of ominous dreams, Balder had begun to fear for his life, whereupon his mother, the goddess Frigg, obliged all living things to promise not to harm her beautiful son. Once this was done the gods, thinking Balder invulnerable, took to throwing things at him for sport.

At this point another god, Loki, enters the story. Loki was the trickster figure of Northern European mythology, progenitor of the wolf-monster Fenrir, the serpent at the base of Yggdrasill, and Hel, the ruler of the underworld. Loki, disguised as a woman, engaged Frigg in conversation, and learned from her that a little plant called the mistletoe had not taken the oath against harming Balder. The evil Loki then plucked the plant, fashioned it into a dart, and gave it to the blind god Hoder to throw at Balder. Hoder did so with Loki's help, and the mistletoe pierced Balder's heart, killing the innocent god. The Aesir fell into a state of grief and despair. A magnificent funeral was held during which Balder and his wife, Nanna, who had died of a broken heart, were burned on a pyre.

Northern mythology is not a happy mythology. Always hanging above everything—even the gods—are the twin specters of death and Ragnarok, the time of the destruction of the world. This apocalypse will be foreshadowed, according to the *Prose Edda*, by a loss of respect for kings and moral standards, and by an epidemic of war, incest, and murder. The sun and moon will be eaten by a monster wolf and the stars will fall from the sky. Finally, the whole earth and the world tree will shake. Loki will lead the giants into battle against the gods; both sides will be destroyed and the world will perish in fire.

As is the case with most mythologies, however, this myth does not end with Ragnarok. It is said that a new, cleansed earth will return to life after the fire and that it will be watched over by the sons of the old gods, led by Balder, who will return from the dead. Furthermore, two humans will have remained sheltered under Yggdrasill, and they will become the parents of a new race of people. Finally, a new sun will blaze forth, larger and warmer than the old one—a welcome thought to the people of the cold north.

Having reviewed some of the major themes of particular ethnic mythologies, we can embark on a voyage through a world mythology that transcends individuals, religions, tribes, nations, and even cultures. Ethnic mythologies are fascinating for what they show us about particular people at a particular time, but to find an answer to the question "What does mythology have to do with me?" we must turn to a cross-cultural approach. Only by means of such an approach—only by releasing ourselves from the confines of chronology and history—will we find the meaning behind the gods who die and come back to life, the gods who contain in themselves infinite love and infinite power, and the heroes who are born of virgins and who descend to the underworld only to return stronger than before.

The Kingdom of the Dead

No mythic history is as perfectly preserved—and imperfectly understood—as that of ancient Egypt. From the great pyramids of Giza, the vast necropolis at Thebes, and the sandy wastes of the Western Desert have come countless representations of that civilization's many gods. All have names but few have identities, for the legends associated with them were handed down by word of mouth—and consequently lost when imperial Egypt collapsed under the combined pressures of internal unrest and external aggression. The oldest of these images date from 3500 B.C., but these are mostly tribal totems; only later, after centuries of anthropomorphic transformation, would the familiar Egyptian pantheon of animal-headed deities emerge. At the head of this pantheon was a prepotent solar deity whose names and manifestations were legion. In association with the falcon-god Horus, an equally ancient sun-god whose right eye was the sun and left eye the moon, this greatest of all Egyptian deities ruled as Ra-Harakhte (above). His crown, a solar disk, shed its beneficent rays upon the pharaoh, his subjects, and the fertile river valley in which they lived. And his principal sanctuary, the sacred city of Heliopolis, was dominated by a giant obelisk said to represent a petrified sunbeam.

The world's oldest extant religious writings are papyri compiled in the third millennium B.C. and known collectively as the *Pyramid Texts*. The repetition of those ritual incantations was thought to ensure the safe passage of a deceased pharaoh on his dark journey to the Kingdom of the Dead, where his mummified remains were guarded in perpetuity by Horus-Ra. The black diorite statue at lower right reveals the falcon-god in his role as guardian, his wings wrapped protectively around the head of Chephren, the "son of Ra" who built the second pyramid at Giza. At left the scale is reversed: King Nectanebo, who ruled under the Persians in the fourth century B.C., is dwarfed by a glowering Horus. The papyrus detail below presents the solar deity in yet another guise, in combination with the Aten, or sun disk, and the *uraeus*, the rampant cobra that symbolized pharaonic power. Of the sun-god's other manifestations, one of the most intriguing is Khepri, the scarab beetle. Like this humble insect—which lays its eggs in a dung ball and then rolls that malodorous nursery before it wherever it goes—Khepri was believed to roll the great ball of the sun across the skies. At right, a pectoral of the New Kingdom period, executed in lapis lazuli and gold, shows the god of the rising sun flanked by his great-granddaughters Isis and Nephthys.

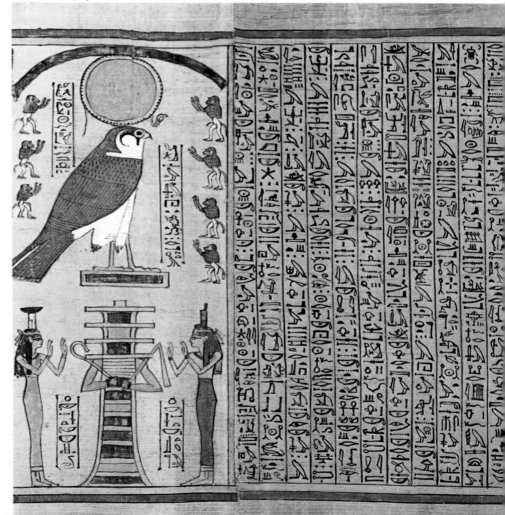

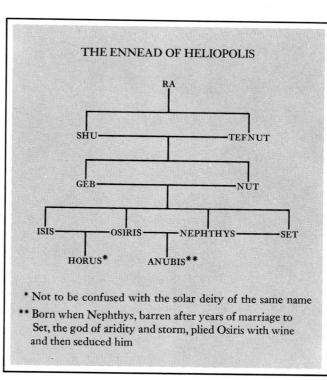

THE ENNEAD OF HELIOPOLIS

```
                        RA
          ┌─────────────┼─────────────┐
        SHU─────────────────────────TEFNUT
          │             │             │
        GEB─────────────────────────NUT
     ┌────┼──────┬──────────────┬─────┐
   ISIS───────OSIRIS────────NEPHTHYS───────SET
          └──────┬──────────────┬──────┘
             HORUS*          ANUBIS**
```

* Not to be confused with the solar deity of the same name

** Born when Nephthys, barren after years of marriage to
Set, the god of aridity and storm, plied Osiris with wine
and then seduced him

As the genealogical chart at left indicates, incest was the favored means of procreation among members of the Ennead of Heliopolis, as the Egyptian pantheon was known. This pattern of sibling intermarriage—a common feature of most Western mythologies, including the Greco-Roman—was harmless at the cosmic level but disastrous at the human. Emulated by Egypt's monarchs, it eventually produced a line of hopelessly inbred, genetically unfit sovereigns incapable of governing their sprawling empire. According to Egyptian cosmology, life on earth began when Ra entered the cosmic void, displacing Nun, the embodiment of chaotic darkness. In time Ra was assigned consorts—among them his own daughters—but early Egyptians believed that the sun-god had created the celestial twins, Shu and Tefnut, "without recourse to woman." Shu, god of the air, was generally depicted in human form, whereas his sister-wife, Tefnut, goddess of dew and rain, was most frequently envisioned as a lioness. This first couple of the Ennead likewise produced twin offspring, the earth-god Geb and Nut, goddess of the sky. Three of these four gods appear on the papyrus seen above, which recalls one of the most famous incidents in Egyptian mythology: Ra, irate when he discovers that his grandchildren, Geb and Nut, have secretly married, sends Shu to separate the siblings on their conjugal bed—thus creating a permanent gap in nature between the green earth and the starry heavens. In his role as the Atlas of Egyptian mythology, Shu, who has insinuated himself between the divine lovers, holds aloft the star-spangled, vastly elongated torso of his daughter, Nut. Geb sprawls at his feet, limbs akimbo to suggest the hilly surface of the earth itself. Space and light fill the void that has been created between the two.

23

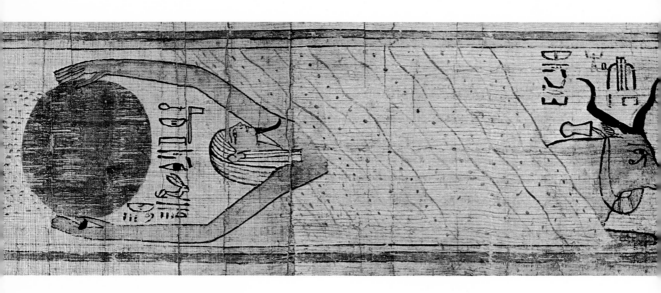

In the three millennia between the unification of Egypt by Narmer and its conquest by Alexander the Great, thirty dynasties superintended life along the banks of the Nile. Each left its impress upon Egyptian cosmology, which grew richer, subtler, and more complex over the centuries. During the Fourth Dynasty, for instance, immortality was conferred upon Imhotep, the architect who designed the first large-scale stone edifice the world had ever seen—the Step Pyramid at Sakkara. Thereafter his mortal origins were ignored and he was worshiped as a son of Ptah, the guardian god of Memphis, and his consort, Sekhmet. And during the Eighteenth Dynasty the epicene and idiosyncratic Akhnaton, frequently identified as the world's first monotheist, briefly proscribed worship of all gods except the Aten, or sun disk. It is hardly surprising, then, that the salient characteristics of a particular deity are often difficult to define, time and changing practice having badly blurred their original outlines. At left, for instance, it is Shu—and not the sacred scarab Khepri—who guides the sun across the sky; and below, at far left, it is Shu's wife, Tefnut, who wears the *sistrum*, a musical instrument more commonly identified with her granddaughter Isis. Their son, the earth-god Geb, is depicted below, center, with one of his several totems, the goose known as "the Great Cackler"—a reminder that one popular myth held that Geb, transformed into a goose, had hatched the sun from an egg. By the height of the imperial epoch such symbolism had become exceedingly elaborate, as the representation below of Hathor as a cow attests. As goddess of the sky she supports the four corners of the earth with her sturdy legs. As the embodiment of music, motherhood, and joy she suckles the infant pharaoh. And as the Lady of the Sycamore Tree she thrusts her head through a wreath of foliage to welcome the deceased pharaoh to the Kingdom of the Dead.

Although the ancient Egyptians recognized more than 740 tutelary gods, some of them little more than tribal totems sacred only to a single village, there was one deity who was worshiped the length of the Nile valley. His name was Hapi, and he was master of the great river itself. It is understandable that all Egyptians should have revered this god of waters, for all depended upon the Nile's annual rise and fall to replenish the rich soil of their valley and, later, irrigate their crops. Hapi, who was exalted above Ra by his followers, was said to dwell on the island of Bigeh near the First Cataract—and to pass through both heaven and hell before emerging from a cavern on Elephantine Island, downriver at Aswan. As the fresco detail at lower left indicates, Hapi was frequently shown as an androgene whose pendant female breasts symbolized the life-giving powers of the Nile. Representations of the blue-skinned god usually depict him clad in the pleated linen breechcloth of a river boatman, his brow crowned with a wreath of aquatic plants. Like all major Egyptian deities, Hapi was believed capable of assuming a variety of zoomorphic forms, among them that of a baboon. As color alone indicates, the bright blue faience figurine below is Hapi in animal guise. The god of the Nile is also associated with the sacred bull of Memphis (opposite), a living fertility emblem whose Greek name was Apis, a corruption of the Egyptian name Hapi. In addition, Hapi was frequently identified with Osiris, god of both death and regenerative life. The latter's annual obsequies occurred when the Nile crested, and his followers often described the Apis bull as a resurrected son of Osiris. Paramount though he was, Hapi was by no means the only river god worshiped by the ancient Egyptians. By the Middle Kingdom period obeisance to Thoth, the ibis-headed god of the Nile delta, was widespread; his devotees extolled him as the patron of the sciences, inventor of writing, spokesman for the gods, and keeper of their records. Another popular river deity was Neith (left), the so-called mother of the gods who was worshiped from predynastic times in the western delta city of Sais.

Among the oldest—and most enduring—of Egyptian gods were those who served as guardians of the great cities of Lower Egypt. The most famous of these tutelary deities was Ptah (above, right), sovereign god of the Old Kingdom capital of Memphis and creator of the physical world. According to Memphite cosmology, it was he who established cults of worship for all the other gods and who dictated what form obsequies to them should take. Often depicted in funerary bandages—perhaps because sculptors of the period were unable to execute articulated limbs—Ptah was shown holding a composite sceptre that united the hieroglyphs for life, stability, and omnipotence. Ptah's consort was Sekhmet (near right), a lion-headed goddess of war. These guardian gods of Memphis were naturally associated with Egypt's rulers, who were crowned in the ancient capital, but the pharaohs enjoyed the protection of numerous other deities as well. Foremost among these was the sun-god Horus (above, left), who also appears on the bas-relief at far right, pressing an *ankh*, symbol of regenerative life, to the lips of the pharaoh. Thebes, the capital of New Kingdom Egypt, fell under the special protection of Amon-Ra (center, right), whose cult became ascendant following the country's second reunification in 1570 B.C. The centuries that followed witnessed a resurgence of temple-building in the name of Amon-Ra. At far right below is the ruined hypostyle of the quarter-mile-long temple of Amon-Ra at Karnak.

28

The most familiar and most quintessential scene in Egyptian mythology is the one illustrated below, the weighing of souls from the *Book of the Dead*. At center: giant scales presided over by Anubis, jackal-headed god of the Kingdom of the Dead. It is he who weighs the heart of the deceased against a feather, symbol

of *maat*, or justice. Behind Anubis stands Thoth, the divine scribe; and behind him lurks Amemait, part lion, part hippo, part crocodile—and ready to devour the hearts of those who fail the test. Above: on-lookers, each representing one of Egypt's provinces, who have come to question the deceased on his previous life.

Both in predynastic times and during the last centuries of the imperial era the veneration of animals took on particular significance in ancient Egyptian life, and in those epochs uncounted thousands of birds, fish, reptiles, and small mammals were interred in the hot sands of the Sahara. These ritual burials, which extended to the lowliest members of the animal kingdom, were often performed with considerable ceremony. An entire crocodile necropolis—complete with mummified eggs and young—has been discovered on the banks of the Nile, for example, and it is said that the pharaohs themselves attended the rites accorded the sacred black bulls of Memphis. The most universally hallowed of birds was the falcon (below), long identified with the pharaoh, but equal respect was accorded the ibis (top, right), totem of Thoth, god of wisdom. Bast, the feline goddess of pleasure (left), was extraordinarily popular in New Kingdom times and whole families were known to go into deep mourning when their sacred cat died. The bronze receptacle at right center, which once encased a mummified snake, is surmounted by a representation of Buto, cobra-goddess of the delta marshes. At lower right is the holy ram Banebdetet, arbiter in a famous quarrel between Horus and his evil uncle, Set.

2

Man, Myth, and History

EVER SINCE MAN first began to be aware of his own mythmaking capacity he has been fascinated by the possibility that myths are riddles which, if solved, can lead to discoveries in other fields—in history, in anthropology, in archaeology. This approach to mythology reached its zenith during the years immediately following the publication of Sir James Frazer's *The Golden Bough* in 1890. Frazer's monumental work dramatically demonstrated the etiological or causal function of mythology—a function that will be illustrated in this chapter by means of several ancient stories, tales that make clear the connections between myth and ritual, myth and shamanism, myth and ancient institution, and myth and pervading religious belief—and myth in relation to natural phenomena, place names, historical incidents, and human nature.

The first of these stories is of Phrygian origin and is very ancient. In simplified form it relates how the Agdos rock, having taken the form of the Great Mother Cybele, is impregnated by the sky-god Papas. In due time the rock gives birth to the savage monster Agdistis. The gods, desperate for some means of curbing Agdistis, who destroys whom and what he chooses, agree to a plan devised by the god of wine. Knowing that Agdistis drinks regularly at a certain stream, this prototypical Dionysus turns the water into wine. Agdistis comes to drink, and he soon falls into a drunken sleep. His genitals are then tied to a nearby tree—so that when he awakes and springs to his feet with his customary compulsion, Agdistis castrates himself. The earth promptly absorbs both the lost parts and the blood, producing the pomegranate tree. Sometime thereafter the daughter of a king takes some fruit from this beautiful tree and places it on her lap—whereupon it disappears and she conceives a child. The king her father, unwilling to believe this first of many tales of immaculate conception, imprisons his daughter in anger at her disgrace. In time the virgin is delivered of a boy child, whom the king takes into the wilderness to die. There the foundling is cared for by a goat, and there the boy Attis develops into a youth so beautiful as to attract the affections of both the Great Mother and the maimed Agdistis. A certain king now arranges for Attis to wed his daughter only to have Agdistis appear in a jealous rage at the wedding and drive everyone mad with the music of a syrinx. Attis thereupon demonstrates his total commitment to the ways of his holy family by doing to himself what had been done to Agdistis—he castrates himself under a pine

Exquisitely wrought in gold and lapis lazuli, a bearded ram peers from a thicket—a Sumerian artist's imaginative depiction of the recurrent tree-of-life symbol.

tree. From his blood spring violets, and in due course Attis himself returns to life.

In ancient Phrygia, and later as far west as Rome, an annual ritual was held to celebrate Attis's death and resurrection. At the end of March a pine tree was cut and brought to the sanctuary of the Great Mother Cybele. This tree was treated like a divine corpse and strung with violets. An effigy of Attis was then tied to the tree, and during a day of frenzied celebration the priests of the cult slashed their bodies while novices castrated themselves. The severed genitals were then buried along with the effigy. These grisly events were followed by a period of fasting and mourning, but when night fell sorrow became joy: the tomb, recently sealed, was opened and revealed to be empty, signaling the resurrection of the god.

It is clear, in this instance, that myth and ritual are intricately related. The general wildness of the ritual is of a kind associated with Agdistis. The celebration of fertility, which is the practical purpose of the ritual and is symbolized by both the pomegranate tree and the violets, is further expressed in the ritual by the literal planting of the seed of Agdistis, Attis, and the novices in the Great Mother. And the presence of the sacred tree in the ritual ties Attis to such other kingly or godly victims as the Babylonian Adonis, born of a tree; the Egyptian Osiris, buried in one; and the Norse Odin, hanged from one. The tree is the tree of life, rooted in the religious unknown. In the modern world a remnant of this symbolism remains in the Christmas tree, a vivid expression of the life that is born anew with Christ.

A second illustration of the explanatory function of myth is contained in a story told by the Cherokee Indians. While hunting in the wilds, the tale begins, an Indian wounds a black bear. The bear moves off and the man continues to shoot arrows at it, but to no avail for the bear is protected by magic. Finally the bear turns to the hunter, pulls the arrows from his body, and says, "It is useless for you to shoot, for you cannot kill me; come and live with me in my house." Together

hunter and hunted enter a cave in the side of the mountain, where other bears are holding council. All kinds of bears are there—old, young, white, black, and brown. The bears sense the presence of the hunter and ask, "What smells bad here?" "Never mind," says their chief, a great white bear. "It is a visitor. Leave him alone."

At this point the hunter and his ursine host repair to another cave in the mountainside. Here the bear's magic works to feed the man. By sitting up and rubbing his stomach the bear can produce quantities of chestnuts, huckleberries, blackberries, and acorns, a diet that sustains both man and beast through the long winter. During these months the hunter grows hair all over his body and begins to learn the ways of the bears. Early in the spring the bear says to the man, "Your tribe is preparing for a great hunt. They will come here to kill me. They will take my clothes—my skin—and they will take you back to your home." A few days later the bear observes, "This is the day your brothers will come—and this is what you must do: when they have killed me, dragged me outside, skinned me, and cut me into pieces, cover my blood with leaves and look back after they have taken you away."

Almost immediately thereafter the hunters come, and all happens as the bear had said it would. The bear is indeed killed, skinned, and quartered, and the man is retrieved from the cave. Before leaving he spreads leaves over the spilled blood, and when he looks back he sees the bear rise intact from the leaves, shake himself, and return to the woods.

On one level this is merely a myth explaining a particular tribe's totem, or sacred animal. Thus the bear in the story is magic; he provides food and protection, which is exactly what a totem is supposed to do. The hunter, who literally grows a bear costume all over his body, and who is chosen by the bear to be trained into his ways, is the shaman, or medicine man, of the cult. His winter in the wilderness is the shaman's traditional period of preparatory withdrawal to learn the arts of his trade.

On a deeper level, however, this bear-man legend is a universal story, one in which the resurrection theme emerges once more from the human psyche. The bear is an especially appropriate symbol here, because each spring bears do indeed arise from the deathlike state of

hibernation. In his ability to read thoughts, in his knowledge of his role as a victim of the tribe, in his instructions to the man, in his desire to protect and teach the very person who has wounded him, and in his miraculous resurrection, the bear is another expression of the myth embodied in all of the culture heroes who die and come back to life.

A third story, this one Indian in origin, illustrates the use of myth to justify existing institutions. On a certain evening the Bodhisattva, the future Buddha, sits down at the foot of the bo tree—the tree of wisdom—and makes the following resolution: "Though my skin, my nerves, and my bones should waste away and my life-blood dry, I will not leave this seat until I have attained Supreme Enlightenment." Mara, the Fiend, now comes to the tree with the intention of breaking the great man's resolve. He first assumes the guise of a messenger sent to the Bodhisattva with news of the overthrow of his father's kingdom, the confiscation of his possessions, and the abduction of his wife. But instead of rushing homeward the future Buddha only sits in contemplation, seeing worldly vice in all the actions taken against him. This causes him to reflect further on the folly of human nature and to confirm the wisdom of his original resolution.

Mara then employs the elements in his attempt to unseat the Bodhisattva, but neither wind, rain, water, a shower of rocks, nor fire budge him. Finally, upon having his reputation as an almsgiver questioned, the Bodhisattva asks the earth itself to attest to his generosity—which it promptly does in a voice of thunder. Mara then uses his own daughters to tempt the hero, but the Bodhisattva eschews the pleasures of the flesh. He has become the Enlightened Buddha, having remained motionless for seven days.

The story of the Buddha under the bo tree, like that of Jesus in the wilderness or Mohammed in the cave, is a story of overcoming the temptation of the flesh through discipline, contemplation, and meditation. It expresses in mythic terms the spirit of what cloistered orders of various faiths have always attempted to achieve in spiritual terms—union with a higher reality that transcends the material world. Thus the

Three additional representations of the tree of life are found in the iconography of unrelated, widely dispersed mythologies: Buddha and the bo tree (left, below); an intricately carved world tree, Yggdrasill, from a Norwegian stave church (near right); Christian man in the tree, with death and hell gaping below (far right).

38

Buddha myth is an "explanation" of both monasticism and mysticism.

Myths were often used to explain natural phenomena as well. A familiar story of this type is that of Demeter, the Greek goddess of agriculture, and her beautiful daughter Persephone. While playing with her friends in a field one day, Persephone is captured and ravished by Hades and taken to the underworld as his wife. Hades is, of course, a personification of death and Persephone of young life. In her grief and anger, Demeter senselessly destroys the earth's crops and brings about a great drought and famine. Zeus now arranges a compromise between Hades, his brother, and Demeter, one whereby Persephone is allowed to return to her mother for two thirds of each year. She cannot return permanently because she has eaten the food of the underworld, the pomegranate, associated mythically—as we have seen in the Attis story —with sexuality. Persephone's fate is, then, a symbol of lost virginity and the consequent impossibility of ever again being merely a child.

Demeter was henceforth to greet the annual return of her daughter with a replenishing of the earth—and mark Persephone's annual descent to Hades with a repetition of the destruction of agriculture. The arrival of Persephone is thus an explanation of spring and summer; her departure, of fall and winter.

Myths have also been used to explain the names of places. Take the story of the unfortunate Io, for instance, beloved of Zeus and disguised by him as a cow in order to put that god's jealous wife off the track. The ever-watchful Hera was not to be fooled, however, and she doomed Io to be chased about the world by a tormenting gadfly. It is said that the Bosporus, which means "cow's ford," and the Ionian Sea were both crossed by the fleeing Io, and both are named for her.

In addition, myths have been used to explain aspects of human nature, or simply to entertain. In Greece, for example, gods and goddesses personified human types, tendencies, and activities. Thus Ares is the god of war, Aphrodite is the goddess of love, and the two become involved in a love affair expressing the truth of the saying, "All is fair in love and war." And when Hephaestus, who has pretended to be out of town, sets a snare that catches his wife, Aphrodite, and Ares in the very act of love—and then arrives with the other gods to mock the guilty pair—we can assume that Greek mythmakers were simply explaining a common enough human occurrence. Implicitly, of course, a lesson is taught by this kind of story, and this, too, is a common function of myths. When Icarus disobeys the instructions of his father, Daedalus, and flies too close to the sun with his waxen wings, the wax melts, his wings fall off, and he falls into the sea and drowns. The lesson is obvious. It is similar to the one contained in the story about Phaeton, who insists on driving the sun chariot of his father, Apollo, and who in the process burns the earth—leaving the Milky Way as a scar—and kills himself. Carved upon his tomb are the lines:

> Here Phaeton lies who drove the Sun-god's car.
> Greatly he failed, but he had greatly dared.

A function of myth that periodically fascinates scholars is the historical function. Those who approach the subject from this direction see in myths reflections of—or metaphors for—actual historical events. Thus, for example, the mythical Trojan War, supposedly fought over Helen, is seen as a glorification of a series of real clashes between the peoples of what is now Greece and those of Asia Minor for control of the Dardanelles—a clash that has since been repeated many times. Occasionally historical mythologists have achieved spectacular results. In the case of the Trojan War, for instance, such theorizing was to lead a nineteenth-century German adventurer, Heinrich Schliemann, to the site of Troy itself.

From early childhood Schliemann's one ambition in life had been to discover the ancient city of Troy, a city most of his contemporaries believed was purely mythical. By the age of forty-one he had made enough money in business to sell out and begin his quest. He studied archaeology in Paris for a time and then traveled to the Dardanelles. This was a mythical body of water if ever there was one; Leander was said to have swam it to visit his beloved Hero, and a modern hero, Lord Byron, had swam it simply because it had a mythical aura about it. Here, not far from the small Turkish village of Hisarlik, Schliemann spotted a mound rising somewhat above a great plain. He excavated—not always with great skill, for like the heroes he sought, he was more possessed than careful—and came upon several layers of ancient urban ruins, one of which could be dated to the period assigned by Greek tradition to the Trojan War. That level showed definite signs of having suffered violent destruction, not at the hands of nature but of man. Schliemann had found his Troy.

Historical bases can be demonstrated for more than a few great mythic events. Noah's Flood has been shown to have a possible factual foundation, corresponding to a great flood that occurred in the valley

History fulfilled myth dramatically in sixteenth-century Mexico. The bearded, fair-skinned Toltec-Aztec god Quetzalcoatl (whose symbol was a feathered serpent, above) had long since disappeared—with the promise he would return from the east to reclaim his power. It was a relatively simple matter, therefore, for the Spanish conquistador Hernán Cortés to assume the deity's role and overthrow the Aztec monarchy; at right, a period Indian drawing of the invincible Spanish conquerors.

of the Tigris-Euphrates—a deluge described, in terms very similar to those of the Old Testament Book of Genesis, in a much earlier flood myth that is confirmed by archaeological discoveries at Ur. And there are those who even claim to have discovered pieces of Noah's ark on Turkey's Mount Ararat. Furthermore, an authentic setting has been discovered for the story of Tristan and Isolde—as well as for that of Saint George and the dragon.

The list of historical, possibly historical, or semihistorical myths is, in fact, long: Atlantis and Tara, Theseus and the Minotaur, King Arthur and his knights of the Roundtable—these are but a few of the legendary places, people, and events that have been shown to have some basis in historical fact. At times the quest for mythic history or historical myth has been so pervasive as to resemble ancient mythic quests themselves. We have Jason and his Golden Fleece, Arthur's knights and their Holy Grail, Moses and his Promised Land. We also have Schliemann and his Troy and Fraser and his Golden Bough—and all involve men of heroic singleness of purpose.

Once in a great while, myth can actually intrude upon documented history, as it did in the case of the Toltec-Aztec god-man Quetzalcoatl. According to Mesoamerican legend, Quetzalcoatl had reigned as king in the golden-age city of Tollan. He had been born of a virgin, had fair skin, and had taught his people arts and crafts. He also discovered maize and invented the calendar. Quetzalcoatl's symbol, and perhaps his original form, was the plumed serpent. At a certain point in his benevolent and glorious reign his dark brother, Tezcatlipoca, arrived in Tollan and drove him away. Before leaving, the great priest-king buried his treasures and burned his palaces. During his flight he stopped at various places—under a tree in Quauhtitlan, where he viewed his own old age in a mirror; in a place where his tears flowed through stone; in another where he made a cross by using his bow to shoot the trunk of a

41

póchotl tree through another *póchotl* tree. At last he came to the sea, where he set sail on a raft of serpents—or so one version of the tale has it. Another says that when he reached the shore he was burned on a pyre, only to rise from the fire as a flock of multicolored birds, his soul transformed into the morning star.

Whatever his earthly end, tradition held that Quetzalcoatl would return from the east with fair-skinned followers, defeat the dark one, and reassume power. Aztec astrologers were unable to predict which calendar cycle would be graced by Quetzalcoatl's return, but they did know the name of the year within the cycle: Quetzalcoatl himself had said he would return during a year whose symbol was "One Reed" (*Ce Acatl*). It was of course only coincidence that Hernán Cortés, who was fair-skinned and came from the sea, should arrive in a One Reed year. But this impossible conjunction of myth and history allowed Cortés—who learned of the coincidence from an Indian guide and who thereafter pretended to be Quetzalcoatl—to subdue a large, well-organized, and powerful civilization. Cortés, with a handful of followers, had conquered the mightiest civilization of the Americas, largely because myth had become history for the Aztec.

One of the most moving of "historical" myths is that of Oedipus, a story that comes to us through ancient legends and more particularly through the plays of Sophocles. The factual basis of this myth has been dramatically, if controversially, uncovered in a book called *Oedipus and Akhnaton* by Immanuel Velikovsky, who, like Schliemann and Frazer, is a modern quester with a heroic obsession.

To understand the search for the real Oedipus we must understand something of the legendary Oedipus. Legend has it that Laius, king of Thebes, brought bad luck to his royal house by introducing homosexual love to Greece. The oracle at Delphi told Laius and his wife, Jocasta, that they would have a son who would one day kill his father and marry his mother. Understandably upset when they did have a son, the parents pierced the child's feet and had him taken into the hills, where he was abandoned and left to die. This was not to be, however, for a passing shepherd took pity on the child, nursed him, and eventually gave him to the king and queen of Corinth, who named him Oedipus, "he of the swollen feet"— an acknowledgment of the fact that the piercing had caused a permanent swelling. The kind and childless royal couple treated Oedipus as their own son and he grew up thinking of them as his real parents. All went well until a casual remark aroused doubts in the young man's mind and led him to the oracle at Delphi. There he was told, as his real parents had been told so long ago, that he was destined to kill his father and marry his mother. Confused and fearful, Oedipus vowed that he would never return to Corinth and those he believed to be his parents. In the course of his self-imposed exile, he came to a place where three roads met and there encountered an arrogant man in a chariot whose driver attempted to force the youth off the road by striking him with a whip. In keeping with the customs of the day, Oedipus reacted by drawing his sword against those who had insulted him and succeeded in killing the driver and his master. The latter, as Oedipus would later learn, was his real father, Laius.

Shortly thereafter Oedipus arrived at the outskirts of seven-gated Thebes, which was at the time plagued by a female sphinx who lived on a cliff and killed anyone attempting to enter the city without answering her riddle. "Who is it that walks on four in the morning, two in the day, and three in the evening?" the sphinx asked Oedipus. "Man," he answered. "As a baby he crawls on four, as an adult he walks on two, and in old age he limps about with a cane." Its riddle solved, the monster died, and rolled off the cliff—whereupon the grateful citizens of Thebes gave Oedipus their throne and their queen.

The new king naturally had no idea that his queen, Jocasta, was also his mother. The couple was happy despite the disparity in their ages, and in time two sons, Polynices and Eteocles, and two daughters, Antigone and Ismene, were born to them.

For years Thebes thrived under the hero-king, but then, quite suddenly, famine and plague visited the city. Asked the reason for the apparent anger of the gods, the oracle at Delphi responded that the murderer of the old king, Laius, remained unpunished in Thebes. By questioning several people, including the shepherd who had originally saved his life, Oedipus came to the realization that the oracle's original prophecy had been fulfilled. Horror-struck, Jocasta hanged herself; and Oedipus, after putting out his own eyes, left Thebes in disgrace, accompanied only by his daughter Antigone. He ultimately died a holy death under the protection of Theseus at the sanctuary of Colonus.

In due time Antigone returned to Thebes, where much had happened. Creon, Jocasta's brother, had allowed Oedipus's elder son, Polynices, to assume his father's throne—with the understanding that he would give up his throne on alternate years to his younger brother, Eteocles. This done, Creon had supported Eteocles in his refusal to relinquish his power to Polynices at the proper time. Polynices, with the help of foreign allies, had attacked Thebes. Seven heroes from each side had fought in single combat at each of the seven gates of the city. The attackers had lost, and Polynices and Eteocles had killed each other. Creon, now absolute in his power, denied proper burial to Polynices, whom he called a traitor to the state. Flying in the face of her uncle's strict orders, Antigone performed the proper rites over her brother's body—and Creon promptly condemned her to death by entombment. Too late he realized that his own son, who loved Antigone, had chosen to be buried with her.

According to Velikovsky, this whole legend can be tied to historical occurrences before, during, and immediately after the reign of Akhnaton, the Egyptian pharaoh known as history's first monotheist. The ties begin with the sphinx, which was an Egyptian export to Greece. During the reign of Akhnaton's father, Amenhotep III, there were to be found at the Egyptian Thebes, capital of both Lower and Upper Egypt, many female sphinxes, placed there by Queen Tiy, Amenhotep's wife. The largest of these was set on a cliff overlooking the city, and there human sacrifices were performed.

This parallel is further supported by Amenhotep's homosexual proclivities, which were, like those of the legendary Laius, well known. The connections with the Oedipus story are likewise obvious; if the

Legend often has a basis in fact, however remote in time or distance. Above, the Greek tragic figure Oedipus confronts the sphinx that guarded the entrance to Thebes; by answering her riddle, he freed the city of this terror and was gratefully proclaimed king. The entire horrifying sequel to this event may have had its origin in the historically documented reign of the Eighteenth-Dynasty Egyptian pharaoh Akhnaton (left).

sphinx was imported by the Greeks, why not the whole story? The facts of the reign of Akhnaton need only be listed for further connections to become clear.

The end of Amenhotep's reign was apparently abrupt, and on succeeding to his father's throne Amenhotep IV changed his name to Akhnaton and mutilated his father's name on all official inscriptions. It also seems clear that Amenhotep's wife, Queen Tiy, functioned as head of state after her husband died and before her son ascended the throne. And perhaps most fascinating of all, tomb paintings of the period depict Akhnaton as having disproportionately swollen thighs. In both Greek and ancient Egyptian the words for leg and foot are the same—and thus *oedipus* can mean "he of the swollen legs" as well as "he of the swollen feet."

Early in Akhnaton's reign, the winged sphinx of Thebes was destroyed—it was probably thrown off the great western cliff as a part of the religious reform movement led by the king. There is also evidence suggesting that Akhnaton then took his mother as a consort, and that they produced a daughter, Beketaten. It is also evident that during Akhnaton's reign the Egyptian state suffered dissension and disintegration. The queen's brother, Ay, allied himself with the priests of the old religion, which had been abandoned by Akhnaton, and together they succeeded in dethroning the king.

Smenkhkare, the son of Akhnaton, reigned for a short while but soon lost the throne to his younger brother, Tutankhamen. Thereafter Smenkhkare and his allies attacked Thebes, and both brothers were killed in the ensuing war. Ay, who was to become the next king, personally supervised the burial of young Tutankhamen, as the valuable objects found in the young king's tomb attest. Smenkhkare, however, seems to have been hastily buried—hurriedly embalmed—perhaps by his half sister Meritaten.

It does seem likely, then, that there is a strong connection between myth and history in this case, as there is in other instances discussed here. And in general it is clear that myths do indeed help to explain ancient practices, beliefs, institutions and natural phenomena, historical names, places, and incidents. Were we to stop here, we would be obliged to conclude that myths are an interesting and even fascinating way of illuminating the past. But to stop here would be to leave out the connection between mythology and present-day reality. We have examined our subject in the museum of the past; we must now examine it in our own lives.

The Mighty Olympians

In the beginning there was Chaos, vast and dark, wrote the Greek poet Hesiod in the eighth century B.C. The father of didactic verse was speaking of the creation of the universe, but he might as easily have been referring to the state of Greek cosmology at the time he composed the *Theogony*. After almost three millennia of cultural development, the Aegean Basin was awash in myth—but as yet it had no unifying mythic tradition. Hesiod's great contribution to the literature of mythology banished chaos and imposed lasting order by classifying and consolidating countless local legends. According to the *Theogony*, a union of earth and sky produced the planet's first inhabitants: the Titans, the Cyclopes, and the Furies—all monstrous apparitions representing the unrestrained forces of nature. The youngest of the Titans was Cronus, and it was he who sired the principal deities of the Greek pantheon—Hades, god of the underworld; Poseidon, god of the sea; and Zeus, supreme ruler of the earth. Mighty Zeus, who grew to manhood in the secluded forests of Mount Ida, beyond the reach of his crazed and bloodthirsty father, ultimately deposed Cronus. This proved the easiest of Zeus's tasks, however, for a ten-year battle with the surviving Titans ensued, and no sooner had victory been secured than Zeus and his siblings faced a new challenge, this time from a race of reptilian creatures known as the Giants. Only when they, too, had been vanquished were Zeus and his consort Hera (above) free to settle atop Olympus, there to preside over the greatest of all mythic pantheons.

The ancient Greeks, who assigned human frailties as well as superhuman strengths to their gods, saw Zeus as both a great law-giver and a great philanderer. His sexual appetite was insatiable, his eye ever-roving, and his amorous adventures legion. Hera was the sixth and last of Zeus's wives, but she was by no means the last of his loves. This latter group included the nymph Leto, whose liaison with Zeus was to provoke the long-suffering Hera to new extremes of vengefulness. Learning that Leto was heavy with child, the wrathful goddess attempted to deny the foolish nymph sanctuary during her final days of confinement. Turned away by one city after another, Leto at last took shelter beneath the waves. Unable to prevent the birth, Hera now sought to protract it by refusing to permit Iris, messenger of the gods, to summon the goddess of childbirth to Leto's side. For nine days and nights the nymph suffered the worst pangs of childbirth; only then would Hera permit her to deliver the celestial twins Apollo and Artemis. The winged Iris, handmaiden of Hera and instrument of her vengeance, is seen directly below, conferring with her seated pa-troness. At right a pallid Leto presents her offspring to their father.

Zeus may have been prepotent on Olympus, but Poseidon was undisputed master of the sea. His cult was highly popular, especially in the maritime cities of the Peloponnesus, where he was recognized as the master of rivers and lakes as well. And although he dwelt in the depths of the Aegean, Poseidon was said to be capable of shaking the earth itself. Indeed, during the war with the Giants (subject of the vase painting at near right) the sea-god was credited with sundering whole mountains with his trident. (The pieces, which fell into the sea, formed the Aegean Islands.) Poseidon, too, enjoyed uncounted dalliances with goddesses and mortal women alike, and his progeny included the Cyclopes Polyphemus, blinded by Ulysses. Another son, the heroic Theseus, was taken prisoner by King Minos of Crete, whose annual tribute from the Athenians included seven sons and seven daughters of prominent citizens. After bragging to his captors that he was Poseidon's son, Theseus was hailed before Minos, who tossed a gold ring into the sea and then commanded Theseus to fetch it back from his father. The impetuous youth promptly dived into the ocean, where dolphins bore him to Poseidon's watery court (vase painting detail at far right). There Amphitrite, the sea-god's consort, returned King Minos's ring to Theseus, whom she then presented with the magical crown that later illuminated the youth's path through the fabled Labyrinth. Poseidon was also related to Apollo, who married one of the sea-god's many daughters. Originally a solar deity—possibly with Asiatic or even Nordic roots—Apollo is one of the most fascinating of all Greek gods, celebrated not only at Delphi but throughout the land as the patron of prophecy. The relief detail above shows Apollo (center) in conversation with Poseidon. Artemis, the virgin huntress, sits to her brother's left.

Unlike the Egyptians, the Greeks had a distinctly negative concept of the afterlife—and therefore Hades, guardian of the infernal regions, was not widely worshiped even though he ranked just below Zeus in the Olympic pantheon. As Pluto, god of agricultural wealth, he was deeply venerated, however, and in this guise he was the focus of one of the most popular of all Greek myths—the abduction of Persephone. According to that legend the strikingly beautiful daughter of Zeus and Demeter was gathering wild narcissus in an open field when she was spied by Pluto, who tossed her in his chariot (opposite) and carried her off to his dark realm. Demeter, in her grief, took refuge at the court of Celeus, king of Eleusis—and before her departure she presented the king's eldest son, Triptolemus, with the first grain of corn and with a winged chariot (below) in which to distribute the benefits of agriculture to mankind. So great was Demeter's sorrow that it killed all growing things until Zeus, fearful that famine would engulf the earth, intervened. At his insistence Pluto was compelled to surrender his flowering bride (enthroned alongside him at right) for two thirds of every year. Persephone's return to the surface of the earth (below, right) brought Demeter great joy, and she caused the trees and fields to bloom again. Each autumn thereafter, Persephone would return reluctantly to the underworld, Demeter would mourn anew, and the earth's verdure would wither and die—a concise, if not particularly scientific, explanation for the repeating cycle of the seasons.

Like Apollo, Aphrodite (top right) was Oriental in origin—a lineal descendant of the Babylonian Great Mother, Ishtar, and the Phoenician fertility goddess Astarte. Although commonly described as the patroness of lovers, Aphrodite's domain was, in fact, all of nature. Not until the classical period did she become clearly defined as a love goddess, and even then she took numerous forms. As Aphrodite Porne she was the incarnation of lust and the protectoress of prostitutes, while as Aphrodite Urania, a celestial deity borne aloft on a goose (opposite), she was the representation of ideal love. It was perhaps inevitable that the goddess's transcendent beauty should arouse jealousies on Mount Olympus, buried antagonisms that abruptly surfaced when Eris, god of discord, tossed a golden apple inscribed "For the fairest" among that fair assembly. Hera, Athena, and Aphrodite all laid claim to the glistering prize—and Zeus, unwilling or unable to resolve the ensuing dispute himself, ordered a mortal, Paris, son of King Priam of Troy, to render a verdict. The three goddesses were then brought before the young prince (seated between two Doric columns in the vase painting detail above). Haughty Hera promised Paris a great kingdom in Asia if he chose her; arrogant Athena assured the Trojan that victory on the battlefield would always be his if he chose her instead. Having nothing else to offer, Aphrodite (far left) loosened the clasps of her tunic in a suggestive prelude to offering the prince the most beautiful of mortal women, the fair Helen, wife of Menelaus. The choice was easy: the golden apple went to Aphrodite. The consequences, however, were disastrous: not content to revenge themselves upon Paris alone, the rejected goddesses Hera and Athena were to encourage the decade-long bloodletting known as the Trojan War. By the time that epic conflict had run its terrible course, Paris and most of his race had perished and hate had all but eclipsed love.

Athena, often described as the most characteristically Greek of the Olympians, is also the deity most clearly associated with prehistoric cult worship. She was said to be the first child of Zeus's first wife, Metis, goddess of wisdom—and news of her imminent birth was greeted with special delight. Ecstasy turned to agony shortly thereafter, however, when Zeus was warned that this child was destined to dethrone him. Panicking, the god swallowed his pregnant wife whole—and almost immediately began to suffer from agonizing pain in his temples. To alleviate Zeus's misery his brother Hephaestus, god of fire, cleaved open that throbbing skull with an axe (above) and Athena emerged. Revered as the patroness of horses and home industries, sculptors and spinners, Athena was principally worshiped as a warrior-goddess (left) and depicted in full armor. Sharing her mother's sapience, she was also associated with the owl (top, left), wisest of feathered creatures.

In Greek cosmology only great heroes retained their identities after death; all other mortals were reduced to evanescent shadows. Possessing corporeal form, heroes could intercede with the gods on behalf of lesser men, and consequently the worship of these demigods became immensely popular throughout Greece. No hero was more idolized than Hercules, the personification of physical strength and purported founder of the Olympic Games. His extraordinary exploits, the basis for an entire cycle of myths, inspired generations of Greek artisans, some of whose products are displayed here. The Twelve Labors of Hercules, familiar to the least lettered of ancient Greeks, involved encounters with the Nemean lion (far right), whose skin rendered the hero invincible; the ravening, flesh-eating birds (top, right) of the marshes of Stymphalus; and the three-headed dog Cerberus (near right), guardian of the gates of the underworld. These labors completed, Hercules was to vanquish the river-god Achelous (above).

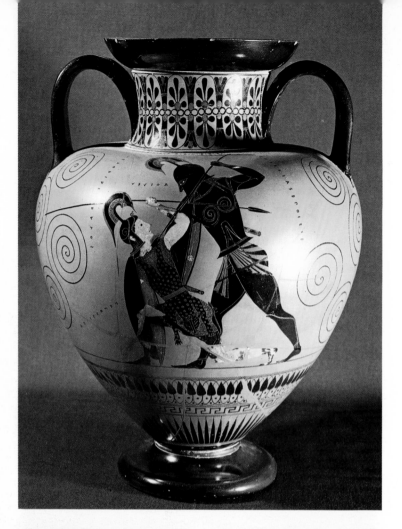

By the eighth century B.C. the cult of the hero had spread throughout Greece, and every major city had adopted its own pantheon of demigods. Athenians, for example, claimed Theseus as their own and delighted in retelling his legend cycle. The red-figure kylix at right, below—a masterpiece attributed to the Codrus painter—offers vignettes from those familiar tales: at center, the slaying of the Minotaur, most famous of Theseus' mythic feats; encircling the rim, glimpses of the hero's earlier exploits, among them the slaughter of the wild sow Phaea and the encounter with Procrustes, whose bed served as a torture rack for unsuspecting visitors. Argos, near Corinth, was said to be the birthplace of Perseus, who is best remembered for his triumph over the most awesome of the Gorgons, snake-haired Medusa. So grotesque was Medusa's visage that merely looking upon her turned men to stone. Perseus therefore approached the Gorgon with his eyes averted, trusting Athena to guide his hand, and lopped off the monster's head with a single stroke of his sickle (below, left). From Medusa's blood sprang the miraculous winged horse Pegasus, whom Bellerophon was able to tame with Athena's help. Astride this steed Corinth's most heroic son was to conquer the tricephalic monster known as the Chimaera (above, right). Achilles, son of Peleus of Thessaly, is renowned today for his vulnerable heel, but in classical Greece he was celebrated as one of the greatest of the nation's military heroes, besieger of Troy and slayer of Hector. The black-figure vase at left, above, shows Achilles poised over Penthesileia, queen of the Amazons and ally of the Trojans.

Part Cretan, part Lydian, and possibly part Vedic in origin, Dionysus was at once the most unusual and most beloved of cult figures. As the god of wine and guardian of civilizing pleasures, Dionysus was naturally popular with celebrants of all ages—so much that later generations tended to de-emphasize his importance as a fertility god. Born from Zeus's thigh and tended in infancy by Hermes, messenger of the gods (far right), Dionysus was to spend most of his adult life carrying vinestock and the secrets of viniculture to distant lands. (The sixth-century kylix painting below is a record of one such journey.) Wherever he traveled Dionysus was accompanied by a ragtag retinue of satyrs, centaurs, and wildly dancing young women such as those adorning the fourth-century vase at near right, above. One of the most intriguing members of the wine-god's entourage was Pan, the cloven-hoofed sylvan piper who was worshiped by the shepherds of Attica because he ensured the fertility of their flocks. The terra-cotta figurine at near right, below, depicts Dionysus himself riding on Pan's totem, a prancing goat.

60

61

It is a widely held belief that the Romans imported their entire mythic tradition en bloc from conquered Greece, assigning new names to an already familiar pantheon in the process. The truth is that temples to the great Olympians were being built in southern Italy even as Rome rose to the north, so that today there are more Doric temples standing in Magna Graecia than there are in Greece itself. It was altogether natural, therefore, for the Romans, who had no coherent mythic tradition of their own, to adopt many—but by no means all—of these foreign deities, to whom they often assigned altogether new personalities. By and large these composite Roman gods were less complex than their Greek counterparts, and many were little more than embodiments of particular virtues. The descendants of Romulus and Remus worshiped a rather restricted pantheon, with veneration most often accorded the so-called Capitoline triad: Jupiter, his consort Juno, and Minerva, goddess of war. Jupiter (above), the supreme Roman deity, was a nature god who came to be recognized as the chief protector of the state. Juno, whose placid features and matronly figure are seen opposite, was a ranking deity in her own right and the protectoress of women. Juno, with her Sabine and Latin roots, was often called the most Italic of goddesses; Minerva, the least. From a very early period Minerva was associated with Athena, the Greek warrior-goddess. Consequently statues such as the one at near left show her in partial armor and holding Athena's owl totem.

The Romans were a bellicose race, and it is hardly surprising, therefore, that the most Roman of their gods should have been the war-god Mars, whose followers outnumbered those of Jupiter himself. As father of Romulus and Remus, Mars had deep associations with the birth of the Roman state; as patron of agriculture and god of spring he had strong ties to the land; and as god of battle he was the spiritual commander-in-chief of the mighty Roman army. The renowned *Ludovici Mars*, opposite, reveals this often savage god in a rare moment of repose. The cherub at his feet indicates that he is thinking not of war but of Venus, the love goddess with whom he is pictured in the fresco detail at top, right. The second level of the Roman pantheon included a plethora of ill-defined and rather insubstantial gods, a number of whom were unidentifiable even as to gender, leading Romans to pray *Si deus si dea*—"Be you god or goddess." Among the better-known deities of this order was Neptune (mosaic detail above), ruler of the sea. Significantly, Neptune inherited the realm but none of the character traits of his Greek counterpart, Poseidon—a common occurrence in cases involving the straightforward adoption of a foreign deity into the Roman pantheon. Interestingly enough, one of the oldest and most purely Latin of gods, Janus, was never depicted in three-dimensional form, as all the adopted Greek gods were. His two faces, which permitted Janus, guardian of the gate, to watch the outside and the inside of city walls at the same time—and simultaneously to protect both the interiors and the exteriors of all Roman houses—are only seen on coins such as the one at right.

In matters of cosmology the principle difference between Greek mythology and Greco-Roman was one of attitude. The Greeks were great embellishers, forever elaborating upon an already rich mythic tradition. The Romans were far more pragmatic, and they were forever stripping their legacy from the Greeks back to its essentials. (Cato the Elder, for instance, viewed all religious obsequies as a "purely contractual" arrangement between individuals and their guardian gods.) Thus, for example, the Romans appropriated the festival of Dionysus wholesale from the Greeks—but chose to inculcate very little of that festival's broader and more significant cultural associations. Reincarnated as Bacchus, god of drink and merry-making, the ancient fertility god of Attica was to achieve immense popularity, especially among the lowest classes of Roman society. The statue at left shows the wine-god with Ampelus, a strikingly beautiful youth to whom Bacchus took a particular fancy. At right, Bacchus's constant companion, the goat-god Pan, appears in relief on a silver disk. The Bacchanalia, most popular of the many official holidays on the Roman state calendar, became an excuse for extended public debauchery—and led to a Senate ban on the festival in 186 B.C. Mere legislation could not suppress Bacchus's cult, however; it simply drove the practitioners underground. Below, a second-century B.C. sarcophagus banded with a Bacchic procession: goat-footed satyrs, a centaur, crazed female Bacchantes dancing with utter abandon, and the aged and perpetually drunken Silenus riding on an elephant.

እዘአባእኩ ውስተ ከርስሃ ታ   የዋህ ለኃጥእት ባመ
ተ ለኖዓ ደቂቀ ታየል ወሴት   ዘ እ ኢትቅሥፈኒ በ
እመ የሐ ልቁ በእይባ እግዚአ   እስመ እማኅፀ እግ
ብሔር መሐሪ ዘእንበለ ቲምም   ብእሲ ንጹሕ ✥

3

The Psychological Perspective

MUCH DISAGREEMENT EXISTS as to how and why similar mythic motifs—the virgin birth, the descent into the underworld, and others—are found in widely separated parts of the world, but two theories vie for favor among scholars. The first of these is the theory of diffusion, which emphasizes the rational or scientific aspects of mythology. The second is the theory of parallel development, which is nearly always associated with the name of the Swiss psychiatrist C. G. Jung and is often disparaged by the diffusionists as being "psychological," "mystical," and "religious."

The diffusionists believe that man's first myths were invented in several culturally ripe mythogenetic zones and were then spread to various parts of the world. In support of this view they point out that a fragment of the Gilgamesh myth has been discovered carved in ancient ruins in South America, that Babylonian tablets have been found among ancient Egyptian artifacts, that Japanese vases have been found in cities built by the Toltecs and Aztecs, that the sweet potato is called *kumar* in Peru and *kumara* in Polynesia. These facts and countless others strongly suggest that myths, like artifacts and alphabets, spread by migration, trade, and conquest.

It would be foolhardy to dismiss the theory of diffusion out of hand, particularly when dramatic proof of its validity is to be found in the following tale: A pious man was warned by heaven to build a giant vessel in preparation for a great flood. He obediently built the vessel, which he then filled with "the seed of all living things." The ensuing deluge set this ark afloat, and it drifted for several days before coming to ground on a mountain. The master of the ark then released some birds, among them a raven—and when this bird did not return, the man knew that the raven had found land. He thereupon made grateful sacrifice to heaven. This is not, as the reader may have thought, the story of Noah but that of Utnapishtim as told in the Babylonian *Epic of Gilgamesh*. The similarity of the two tales does suggest how common the flood myth is in all parts of the Near and Middle East—and, in fact, in corners of the world where floods do not occur.

The case for diffusion—and against the parallel development of myths—could rest here, but for the fact that the flood myth and many other much-repeated motifs existed in the ancient world in places to which migration of these motifs seems unlikely if not impossible. The mistake that many scholars have made is to assume that because diffusion can be demonstrated there cannot also be parallel development. Behind this mistake lurks another false assumption: the diffusionist often considers myths to be nothing more than superstitions passed along from one group to the other. The truth is, of course, that myths can be spontaneous psychic expressions of human aims, apprehensions, and values. The human body is much the same all over the world; so is the human psyche. It follows that if myths are expressions of psychic reality, the most important ones will occur virtually everywhere.

Thus even if a myth can be shown to have been conveyed by traders from one place to another, we must consider why it, as opposed to some other myth, gained acceptance. Whether a certain Aztec myth was inherited from the Chinese, the Egyptians, or the Polynesians is of secondary importance; the point is the Aztecs incorporated the foreign theme because it struck a chord already present in their group psyche. The flood story, for example, is meaningful to all cultures—even to ones with no experience of actual floods—because it expresses a real psychic need of the human spirit to feel it can survive in the face of great and sometimes seemingly irrational natural forces.

When a psychoanalyst studies his patient's dreams over a period of time he is looking for patterns, for recurring images, ideas, or symbols that shed some light on the personality of the dreamer. In this process he will confront several layers of reality. He will learn from conversations with his patient that much of the dream material can be traced to recent events. People, places, and incidents experienced in daily life naturally comprise the most common elements of dreams, for these are the materials closest to the surface of his mind and, therefore, the ones most accessible to him. Moving a level deeper into dreams the analyst confronts patterns unique to the patient in question, patterns that can be traced to heredity and environment. This is the level of the personal unconscious, the so-called Freudian level.

The analyst with an anthropological bent will proceed next to a cultural or societal layer, one that reflects the traditions and concerns of the dreamer's class or group. Finally, analysts willing to look still further will often find motifs or symbols that seem to have no particular source in the dreamer's conscious experience but that nonetheless recur with frequency in his dreams. The logical assumption is that these last symbols, or the impulses expressed by them, are inherited from the human past and reserved in the deepest reaches of the mind. The implicit assumption here is that we inherit psychic characteristics from our ancestors just as we inherit physical ones. And it is because of this collective unconscious, or racial memory, that people of differing cultural backgrounds can respond in the same way to certain motifs or archetypes in literature, music, and art.

The comparative mythologist follows much the same approach, focusing upon a particular mythic story and delving into it layer by layer. On the first level, he attempts to discern concerns peculiar to the time the myth was told in its present form. (Perhaps the tribe was experiencing a bad drought at the time, and thus images of dryness pervade the myth.) Continuing his exploration, the mythologist finds patterns that express the culture of the society as a whole—the way it views the role of women, for example. Finally, he discovers archetypes that transcend the particular culture. Just as the psychoanalyst compares dreams to lay bare the inner nature of an individual, so the mytholgist compares myths to expose the inner nature of the human race. Myths, then, are the dreams of mankind, as the following tale, told by the Tewa Indians of North America, suggests:

Once upon a time there was a beautiful maiden who had refused to marry. Instead, she remained at home with her mother, a maker of water jars. One day the mother asked the daughter to mix the clay for the jars while she went to fetch some water. As the maiden mixed the clay with her feet, some of it entered her and made her pregnant. In time the maiden gave birth —not to a child but to a water jar. Although this angered the girl's mother, her father was oddly pleased and grew to love the little jar. He watched it grow, noting that in a mere twenty days it had become big enough to play with the other children and had learned to talk. Everyone loved the jar, which they dubbed Water Jar Boy. Still, his mother grieved because he had no legs or arms and had to be fed through the jar mouth.

When winter came, Water Jar Boy asked permission to accompany the men of the tribe on the annual rabbit hunt, but his grandfather reminded him, "you can't hunt rabbits; you have no arms or legs." "Never mind," said the jar boy, "you are old and can't catch anything anyway; take me." He soon tracked down a rabbit and, while rolling after it, bumped against a rock. Out of the broken jar sprang a fine boy, fully garbed in Indian clothes and jewelry.

Water Jar Boy now returned to his grandfather, who naturally did not recognize him. "Have you seen my grandson anywhere?" the old man asked.

"I am he," the boy said.

"You are teasing me. My grandson has no arms and legs; he is a jar."

"I am not teasing; I am your grandson. Today, when you let me chase the rabbit, I rolled against a rock, my skin was broken, and I came out. I am your grandson and you must believe me!" The old man, accepting the story, led his grandson home.

The Babylonian hero Gilgamesh is crafted in terra-cotta at left; below, right, a woodcut from a fifteenth-century German Bible adds beguiling if inauthentic mermaids to the legend of Noah.

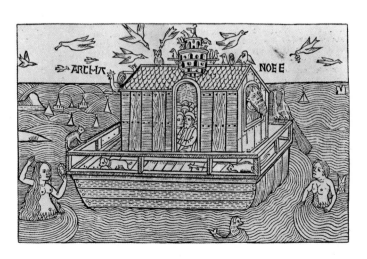

Two mosaics from the Basilica of San Marco in Venice present initial and concluding episodes in the well-known Noah story: at left, the patriarch assists pairs of fowl into the ark; at right, he releases the dove which will return with evidence that dry land has once more emerged from beneath the waters.

When her father returned with the handsome young man, the maiden blushed with embarrassment, thinking the man was a suitor. "This is our Water Jar Boy," said the grandfather, and he told the whole story to the woman. When the old man's tale had been told, Water Jar Boy asked his mother the question no one had answered: who was his father? Told that his mother did not know, the boy declared, "Then I will find my father myself, and I will do it tomorrow."

His mother begged him not to go, but the boy could not be dissuaded. The very next day the boy set out alone for Horse Mesa Point, where he located a natural spring. Not far from the spring was a man who asked the boy where he was going.

"To the spring."

"Why there?"

"To find my father, who lives in this spring."

"You won't find your father there."

"I'll go there; my father lives in the spring."

"Who *is* your father?" the man demanded. The boy paused.

"I think *you* are my father," he declared.

"How do you know?"

"I just know!" the youth insisted.

"You're right," said the man. "I came from the spring to meet you." They embraced and entered the spring, where a number of relatives welcomed the boy.

After a night in the spring Water Jar Boy returned to his mother and told her of his experience, but soon thereafter she became sick and she died.

"I must return to the spring," the boy thought. Reentering the waters, Water Jar Boy encountered his mother, seated alongside his father, whom he now learned was Red Water Snake. "I could not live above the surface of the water," explained the Snake, "so I made your mother join me here." From that time they all lived happily together.

The first thing to be noted in this myth is its dreamlike quality. A

child is born as a water jar; the jar learns to walk and talk. Here is the distortion of reality we have come to expect in dreams. Here is also the dream level that reflects the mundane aspects of Indian culture: springs and water holes, the deadly bite of the water snake, the clay pots used to fetch water from the springs where the snake dwells. Next we move to the Freudian level: the unwanted pregnancy pawned off as a miracle, the quest for approval from the father, the son's search for the father, the rites of passage.

At a still deeper level, this story bears striking similarities to well-known myths. First there is the miraculous conception, which reminds us of Attis, Jesus, and other mythic heroes. Second, there is the breaking of the water jar, signifying childhood initiation. It is the thematic equivalent of Odysseus slaying his first boar or Arthur pulling the sword from the rock. The fact that Water Jar Boy reaches adolescence in a mere twenty days reminds us of certain feats achieved by Hercules in his cradle and of the precociousness of the Buddha. Finally, by entering the spring and returning successfully from it, Water Jar Boy emulates Odysseus, Jesus, Dionysus, and many other heroes who descended to the underworld. This story of Water Jar Boy is much more than merely an Indian legend; it is another expression of the concept of the hero, who represents something common in men's psyches.

It should be clear by now that the word "myth," in its deepest sense, differs substantially from the popular concept of myth or mythic story. The stories of Jesus, Attis, Dionysus, and Water Jar Boy have considerable merit as narratives, and might well have survived on their anecdotal charm alone. But the ultimate meaning of these stories is psychological rather than concrete, and the stories themselves serve only as metaphors for the myth, expressing something that is deeply felt but not easily said. Myth, in this sense, has been compared to music—both involve a form of communication that transcends articulated language. The mythologist Claude Levi-Strauss has said, "Music and mythology confront man with virtual objects whose shadow alone is real."

The search for myth, then, is a search for that which is most universally human within material that is often personal or historical in origin. Before all else it is the search for the world hero, who is bent on finding what Samuel Taylor Coleridge called "the infinite I AM." To really understand myth in general—and the myth of the World Hero in particular—one must think of myth not as falsehood or superstition but as an expression of primeval reality, as a revelation of what many would call the sacred.

The Indian mystic and mythologist Ananda Coomaraswamy called myth "the penultimate truth, of which all experience is the temporal reflection." Implicit in this view of myth as something more real than real is the assumption of a relationship between mankind and something beyond the material world—and a consequent assumption that myth reflects that relationship and therefore is, in the broadest sense, religious. In such a view myth becomes the very soul of man—our deepest vision of ourselves in relation to being itself. As such, myth is of immense importance to our psychic lives. The poet Archibald MacLeish has observed:

> A world ends when its metaphor has died. . . .
> It perishes when those images, though seen,
> No longer mean.

To lose conscious contact with the great mythic themes is, then, to lose that which potentially ties humans to one another. To lose consciousness of myth is to open ourselves to false ideologies masquerading as myth: the "myth" of a technocratic solution to our problems, the "myth" of race, the "myth" of the machine.

As the record of our common identity as human beings, real myth —as opposed to mere ideology—provides us with a means of communication that transcends languages, neuroses, cultures, traditions, histories, and religions. This is evident in the very origins of the word "myth." Myth comes from the Greek *mythos* and the root sound *mu*, meaning to mumble, to make a sound with the mouth. "In the beginning was the Word, and the Word was with God, and the Word was God"—in the Judeo-Christian tradition. "The Tao" had a similar meaning for the ancient Chinese, "Brahma" for the Hindu. The "word" in this sense is the ultimate expression of imagination, the ultimate myth. "And the Word was made flesh and dwelt among us," in the many forms of the culture hero—the "hero with a thousand faces" who is, as we shall see in the next chapter, eternal man.

Sage, Saviour, and Prophet

The cult of the hero is almost as old as civilization itself, for even primitive man recognized that his survival in an alien and often hostile world depended upon the courage and resourcefulness of his chosen leaders. It followed, then, that each tribe should revere its own hierarchy of culture heroes, celebrating the skill and bravery of those individuals in story, dance, and song. As these cultures grew more sophisticated and their histories more complex, the elders charged with preserving the tribe's oral tradition began to consolidate and embellish that history, investing some of their predecessors with wholly mythic qualities. In time this process was to transform valorous warriors into invincible demigods and venerated sages into idolized divinities. This latter category includes the founders of three of the world's great religions—Buddhism, Christianity, and Islam. Buddha, Christ, and Mohammed were actual historical personages, but over the centuries their identifiable personal characteristics have gradually been enveloped in the miasma of pure myth. By the tenth century, for instance, when the delicately tinted Sung dynasty Chinese painting above was created, the Buddha had lost all traces of his mundane personality and had assumed a completely mythic identity.

Gautama Buddha, the princely founder of the sect that bears his name, lived a life of asceticism and preached a doctrine of simplicity. He conducted his forty-five-year ministry on the Indian subcontinent, however, among highly superstitious peoples with a well-developed fondness for fables. As a result, mythic attributes were ascribed to the wandering mendicant even before his death in 483 B.C., and shortly thereafter the historical Buddha was entirely subsumed by an exuberant mythic tradition that was largely at odds with the dogma he had espoused. It was said, for instance, that the Buddha's mother, Queen Maya, had conceived miraculously (top, left) when a white elephant bearing a white lotus in his trunk had entered her womb while she slept. At the actual moment of conception, musical instruments played without being touched and rivers stopped flowing. A group of sixty-four Brahmins, summoned by King Suddhodana to interpret his wife's vision, declared that she would bear a male child who would one day rule the world. The future Buddha's birth was also said to have been attended by miracles. While the queen stood under a sal tree in the royal gardens, her womb became transparent and a son emerged from her side (center, left). He leapt nimbly to the ground, and as his feet touched the earth lotuses sprang up beneath him. Seven days later the aged queen died—legend says of pure joy. She left behind the infant son she had named Siddhartha, and he grew to manhood in a luxurious palace on India's border with Nepal (where the bust of Siddhartha seen at right was created). In time the heir-apparent to Suddhodana's throne was to take a wife, the lovely and loyal Yasodhara, born at the same instant the prince was and predestined to be his consort. She soon presented her husband with a son, thus securing the line of succession. (The Buddha would later preach that it was the sacred obligation of every man to produce a son before taking leave of his family to seek the path to enlightenment.) Free at last to abandon the pleasures of the palace for the travail of the pilgrim trail, Siddhartha bade farewell to Yasodhara and their son, Rahula (bottom, left). As he did so he told Rahula that the latter's inheritance would take the form of spiritual rather than worldly wealth.

77

Having heard it prophesied that Siddhartha would choose asceticism over kingship if he were ever to witness old age, sickness, or death—or encounter a true ascetic—Suddhodana kept his son confined to the upper floors of the royal palace. Abetted by the gods, who bore him silently past the sleeping guards at the palace gate, Siddhartha was able to make four separate forays into the surrounding town (near right). The decrepitude and disease he encountered there disturbed him deeply, and shortly thereafter he renounced his throne, shaved his head, donned monk's robes, and set out in search of spiritual fulfillment. After seven years of wandering Siddhartha reached the town of Uruvela, where he sat down beneath a sacred bo tree, vowing not to move or eat until he had achieved enlightenment. For the next twenty-eight days a host of evil spirits, led by the conniving Mara, tried to distract the by now emaciated mendicant (far right) from his vigil, but to no avail. Even Mara's seductive daughters, Discontent, Delight, and Thirst (above), were unable to deflect the future Buddha from his purpose. Having resisted all forms of earthly temptation, Siddhartha achieved *bodhi*, or perfect enlightenment.

Two paths now lay open to Gautama Buddha: he could choose to preach his Eight-fold Path of Enlightenment to others, or he could seek personal salvation. Mara urged the latter, selfish course, but the Buddha, endowed with superhuman powers that permitted him to leap rivers and charm serpents (near right), chose instead to take his message to the peoples of the subcontinent. It was the Buddha's conviction that a combination of correctness in belief, word, and conduct could lead any man to enlightenment, and he began preaching this doctrine in the Deer Park at Benares. "Discover the middle path that leads to rest, to knowledge, to enlightenment and nirvana," he averred in this first sermon, establishing from the first the principal tenets of Buddhism: moderation and charity. (The anonymous eighth-century Chinese painting opposite shows the Buddha seated in lotus position beneath the sacred bo tree, discoursing with an assembly of monks and bodhisattvas.) Having carried his message to every corner of India, the eighty-year-old sage journeyed to Kusinagara, where he came upon a grove of sal trees blooming out of season. There he lay down, and there, attended by the oldest of his disciples, he quietly expired. After lying in state for six days (below), the Buddha's body was placed atop an enormous funeral pyre. All human efforts to ignite the pyre failed, but at the appropriate moment the fire kindled itself spontaneously, reducing the venerated sage's earthly remains to ashes. As the flames leapt up, high winds swept the sere Indian plains, rivers boiled, and the Buddha's departed soul entered directly into nirvana.

It is written in the *Protevangelium*, an apocryphal text attributed to James, the older brother of Jesus of Nazareth, that the latter was born in a cave in the hills outside Bethlehem. No angels attended the birth, and no Eastern potentates—although another brother, Samuel, was able to summon some passing shepherds to the scene. Since that time a tissue of myth has completely enveloped the historical Jesus, whose miraculous conception is said to have been announced by the archangel Gabriel (medieval ivory book cover at left). It is the legendary aspects of Jesus' life that are emphasized in the incomparable fresco panels below and on the following pages. Part of the cycle created by Giotto for the Arena Chapel in Padua, they include the Nativity (below, left) and the presentation of the infant Jesus at the Temple (below).

Jesus of Nazareth's first adherents were the *am ha-aretz*, or "people of the land," who revered him for his healing powers, for his capacity to reduce complex moral issues to lucid parables, and for what the disciple Mark called his "impression of authority." Jesus' ministry among these unlettered and unaffected Palestinians was brief, lasting less than three years. Its enormous and enduring impact was due, in part, to the proselytizing of John the Baptist, said by some to be Jesus' cousin. During the years that the latter toiled as a carpenter in Nazareth, the former walked the length and breadth of the Jordan valley, preaching of the second coming of the Messiah and baptizing converts in preparation for that event. At the beginning of Jesus' ministry John was even to baptize the thirty-year-old Saviour himself (above, left). The details at left, from a fifth-century ivory diptych, illustrate instances of the Nazarene's healing powers. At far left, a lame beggar discards his cane; at near left, a leper is cured by Jesus' touch. The Giotto panel above shows the revivified Lazarus, still in his funerary bandages, reunited with his grieving kinsmen.

Although they had been conquered in 63 B.C. by Pompey's legions, the Jews of Palestine had never fully submitted to their Roman overlords. They staunchly resisted the worship of foreign idols and they refused to accept the puppet Herod, a convert to Judaism, as their true king. And thus when a man some called "the King of the Jews" entered Jerusalem (below) to celebrate Passover, the feast of Jewish liberation, his arrival aroused considerable apprehension. The Nazarene was already known as a preacher of revolutionary doctrines, and when he turned the usurers out of Solomon's Temple he confirmed suspicions that he was an advocate of violent reform as well. To quell the unrest that Jesus' presence aroused, the Romans and their minions sentenced him to die by crucifixion (right, above) on a hill outside the city. Christ's resurrection (right, below) is said to have occurred three days later.

Abdulqasim Mohammed ibn Abdulla ibn Abd al-Mutallib ibn Hashim was as unlikely a candidate to foment a religious revolution as can be imagined. Although he was a member of the illustrious Hashim family, guardians of the sacred Kaaba in Mecca, he himself was destitute and illiterate—an orphan from the age of six who did not even begin his ministry until he was forty. At the time of Mohammed's birth in A.D. 570 the only shared Arab institution was the Kaaba, a rudely constructed stone structure in the heart of Mecca that housed some 360 tribal totems. (In one corner of this holiest of holies stood the legendary Black Stone.) After a childhood spent among sheepherders and camel drivers (left, above), Mohammed married a rich widow and prospered as a merchant. Distressed by the poverty, ignorance, and superstition around him, Mohammed took to meditating for hours at a time—and during one of these vigils he received his calling. He preached the new doctrine in secret for several years, and then in 612 began proselytizing openly. His heretical views soon antagonized the rulers of Mecca, whose plot to murder the Prophet was thwarted by the archangel Gabriel (below), who urged Mohammed and his friend Abu Bakr (below, left) to flee to Medina.

July 2, 622, the date of the Hegira, or flight to Medina, traditionally marks the beginning of the Moslem era. For the next eight years Medina was to serve as the nexus of a rapidly expanding religious empire. There the Koran was committed to memory by the Prophet's numerous disciples and copied onto parchment by highly dedicated scribes. There Mohammed was to perform the modest miracles—such as extracting milk from a dry goat (left, below)—that are associated with this least mythic of religious heroes. There the Prophet himself was to build the first of the mosques (opposite) that were soon to proliferate through the Arab world. And there Mohammed and Abu Bakr (left, above) were to mount a civil war against Mecca. A handful of followers had accompanied the Prophet on his Hegira; ten thousand were to join him when he returned to Mecca in 629 to rededicate the Black Stone of the Kaaba to Islam. Henceforth the fractious, licentious Bedouin would be bound to a temperate life, a single god, and a solitary purpose —the conversion of all other peoples to the creed of the Prophet. Tens of thousands of converts to Islam were obliged to observe what Mohammed called the five pillars of religious duty: regular profession of faith, daily prayer, fasting in the month of Ramadhan, pilgrimage to Mecca, and payment of the *zakah*, a tax to support the poor and the mosques. To these five duties many Moslems added a sixth: *jihad*, or holy war against the nonbeliever. "War is ordained," decreed the Koran, and those words inspired Arab armies to extend Allah's domain from the Indus to Iberia, offering each of their captives the same four alternatives: conversion, tribute, imprisonment, or death by the holy sword of Islam.

أبي طالب سعد بن أبي وقاص سعيد بن عمرو بن زيد

طلحة بن عبد الله زبير بن عوّام ابو عبيدة عامر بن جرّح

عبد الرحمن بن عوف حمزة بن عبد المطلب عبد الله بن

مسعود عمّار بن ياسر صهيب رومي بلال حبشي

The substantiated episodes of Mohammed's life are manifold, making him the most human and least mythological of the three great religious leaders considered in this special section. Even so, the Prophet's life is not without legendary accretions, the most spectacular of which is the famed Vision of the Night Journey to Jerusalem. Drawing upon an isolated allusion to Jerusalem as "the further mosque" in the Koran, Moslems have embroidered a mythic tale so fanciful that it rivals any in the Bible. According to this legend, Mohammed made his journey from Mecca to Jerusalem astride al-Burak, a phantasmagorical winged creature with the face of a woman (above). Alighting upon the sacred rock that stood at the center of Solomon's Temple, the last of Allah's prophets met with his renowned predecessors, among them Abraham, Moses, Solomon, and Jesus. After praying in a grotto below the rock, Mohammed and the archangel Gabriel ascended directly to heaven on a beam of sunlight. Brought into the presence of Allah himself, the trembling Prophet prostrated himself before his maker's burnished throne (opposite) and there learned firsthand of the duties his followers would be expected to perform. Mohammed then retraced his steps, arriving back in Mecca before daybreak. Considering the strictures against license and indulgence that are imposed by the Koran, the Moslem heaven to which Mohammed ascended was a remarkably sybaritic place. Its topmost tier —Seventh Heaven—was graced by seventy-two seductive, sloe-eyed *houris*, maidens whose very presence added an undeniably carnal note to the Moslem's prospects for bliss in the hereafter.

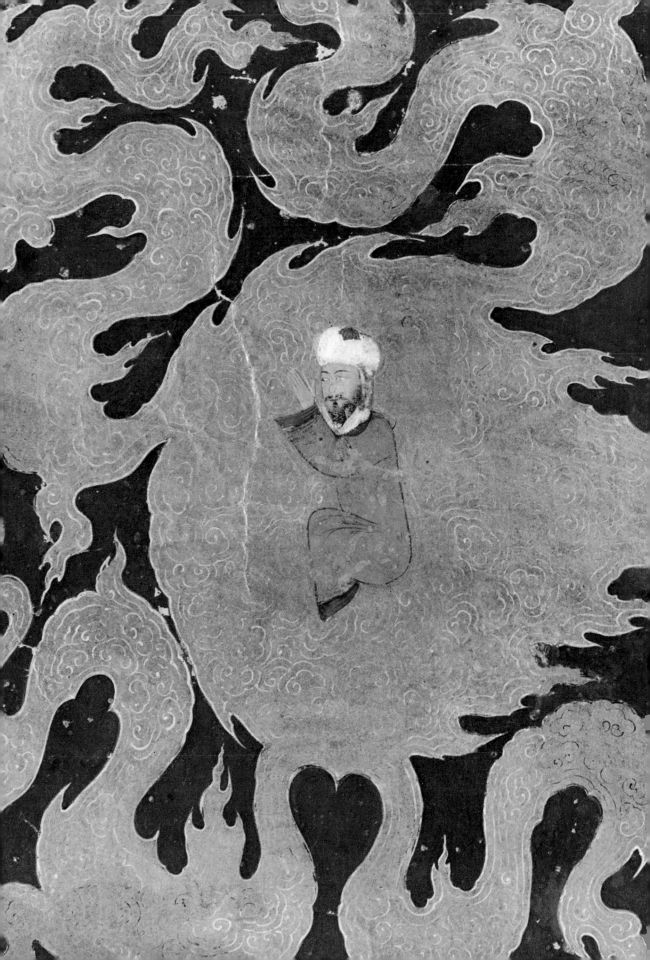

TEMPLVM APOLLINIS

ACHATES   AENEAS   SIBYLLA

NIVMERAIADLIAIENCUMUIRGOPOSCERELFAIA
APUSAITDEUSICCIDIUSCUITALIAFANII·
ITTORESSUBITONONUULTUS·NONCOLORUNUS·
NCOMLTINEMANSERICOMAISDEICIUSABHILUN
LADITILTRACORDA · LIMENIMMAIORQUIUIDERI
CMOMALISONANXXDELATAESTNUMINIQUANDI

4

The Hero with a Thousand Faces

WHEN ODYSSEUS STANDS in the prow of his boat and shouts, "Cyclops, if anyone ever asks you who put your eye out, tell him it was Odysseus, raider of cities, Laertes' son, who did it," he is merely articulating the values of a culture in which survival depended on patrimony, looting, and acts of individual bravado. As recorded by Homer in the *Odyssey*, Greek civilization in the first millennium B.C. was an individual-oriented culture, not a stratified, interdependent culture such as that of Periclean Athens or Augustan Rome. In such a culture Odysseus could boast shamelessly of his exploits and remain a hero, just as Achilles could stoop to dragging the dead Hector around the city of Troy and remain a hero.

There are several basic types of culture hero, the one who represents the shared values of an entire nation being the most common. Thus George Washington's throwing a silver dollar across the Potomac is peculiarly American, perhaps because a dollar has more symbolic significance to Americans than, say, a javelin. In much the same way, Abe Lincoln's reading late into the night by the light of a single candle expresses a passion for self-improvement through self-education that is uniquely American.

One of the earliest of these national heroes was Aeneas, protagonist of the Roman poet Vergil's great epic, the *Aeneid*. Trojan rather than Greek by birth, Aeneas symbolized the Romans' deviation from what they considered corrupt Greek traditions. Unlike Odysseus, Aeneas is pious rather than egotistical—more a priest than a hero, as American poet Ezra Pound noted. This follows rather logically, for whereas Odysseus represented a culture whose values rested upon individual know-how and prowess, the Roman Empire depended upon cooperation and obedience. Odysseus, so fiercely independent, would have posed a clear threat to such a system; Aeneas, ever dutiful, did not. Indeed, his every action sustained and advanced the collective goals of the Romans.

On another level, the priestly Aeneas sets the stage for heroes who represent religions rather than nations. Consider Jesus of Nazareth and Gautama Buddha, for instance; both eschewed the limited, purely nationalistic goals of Odysseus and Aeneas. The victory to which they aspired was achieved by denial of the things of this world, and by turning the other cheek rather than by fighting. The hero, then, can

Among the West's earliest and best-known national heroes is Aeneas, protagonist of Vergil's Latin epic, the Aeneid. *In the fifth-century illustration seen opposite, Aeneas and his faithful companion Achates arrive at the Temple of Apollo at Cumae to consult the famed sibyl there.*

be special in that he represents values directly opposed to those already established in a culture.

Occasionally culture heroes combine religious and national impulses. Joan of Arc is perhaps the supreme example of this type; so in his own way is Mao Tse-tung. Mao is, above anything else, an ideological hero, and he has been endowed by the Chinese with qualities that can only be called heroic. He is esteemed as an infallible teacher; he is revered as the leader of the Long March, itself a near-mythic event; he is widely believed, even in old age, to be capable of swimming impossible distances in the sacred Yangtze; and he feeds the multitudes while transforming a culture.

The true culture hero is the medium for the language of myth; his life is what mythologist Joseph Campbell has called "the wonderful song of the soul's high adventure." During his lifetime this hero repeatedly tests himself in a series of adventures that also serve to establish his identity. These adventures may be national, religious, cultural, or ideological, but at their deepest level they are also psychological. When Odysseus searches for a way home, Jason for the Golden Fleece, and Jesus of Nazareth for the Kingdom of God they are all, consciously or unconsciously, searching for the meaning of life. In the process they have broken through the barriers erected by their particular cultures and become universal human figures. For this reason Theseus' story could have been understood by the Aztecs—and Quetzalcoatl's by the Greeks—because at the psychological level, at the level of basic myth, they are the same story. The agony of their quests reflects the agony of man's emotional and spiritual growth.

We turn now to the great heroic myth, the "monomyth" itself. The epic hero's life, the framework for this myth, can for convenience be divided into eight parts: birth, initiation, withdrawal, quest or trial, death, descent to the underworld, rebirth, and apotheosis or reunion with the unknown. And if we accept the assertion that culture heroes are but various guises of a single world hero, then the parts of the great heroic myth can be illustrated by stories from all over the world. Take, for example, the story of the Indian hero Karna, whose birth is recorded in the ancient Hindu epic the *Mahabharata*. Karna's mother, fearful that she might prove barren, prayed with such devotion to the family gods that she attracted the attention of the wise Durvasa, who taught her a spell whereby she might conceive. She obediently invoked the great sun-god, he who sees all things, and by the "light of the universe" she conceived a son who was born clothed in armor and earrings. Afraid of what her friends and relatives would think, she threw the newborn child into the river, from whence he was retrieved by a charioteer and his wife. The couple adopted the boy, who grew into a fine young man and fervent worshiper of the sun-god. And therefore when the god asked for alms, the young man cut the armor from his body and the earrings from his ears and offered these objects. This act earned him the name Karna, "the Cutter."

We note, then, that the world hero is born in a miraculous manner. Often—as in the case of Quetzalcoatl, Jesus, Attis, and Water Jar Boy as well as Karna—he is born of a virgin. In many cases he is also abandoned to the elements at birth. This is true in the case of Karna; it also applies to Oedipus, to Moses, to the great German hero Siegfried, to the ancient Babylonian king Sargon, and to many others. From this abandonment, the highborn hero is rescued by people of the lower classes—or, less frequently, by animals. Romulus and Remus, for example, were raised by a wolf; Attis, by a goat. Siegfried was adopted first by a doe and only later by a blacksmith. Animals and shepherds also play a role in Jesus' nativity story.

Sir James Frazer hypothesized that the concept of the virgin birth could be traced to primitive man's failure to understand the connection between intercourse and pregnancy. Although many question Frazer's assumption, it is true that this concept accurately conveys the sense of awe that has always attended the processes of conception and childbirth.

There are other, equally compelling reasons for the widespread popularity of the virgin birth motif. Since the beginning of time, or at least since the time represented by the story of original sin and the expulsion from the Garden of Eden, man has sought a saviour-hero or messiah untarnished by human failings. Such a hero must necessarily be conceived as the first man had been, out of the void. Thus Jesus was said to be immaculately conceived, the Buddha was alleged to have been born "unsmeared by any impurity from his mother's womb," and the Persian man-god Mithras was born—on December 25—like Agdistis, of a rock.

The fact that the child is abandoned to nature is a further ratification of his universal origins and his universal nature. He is given back to the Great Mother—to the maternal river, from which he is retrieved by an ordinary human being; to the flow of life, from which he is adopted by us all. He is no one's property, not even his mother's. And so it is that when Mary scolds the young Jesus for remaining behind in the temple he reminds her that he belongs not to her but to God. "Mother, what have I to do with you?" he asks. From the very beginning the hero must move away from local ties, must learn the universal language of myth in order to more fully embody the Word.

On the threshold of manhood this hero must endure some form of initiation in order to be recognized for what he is. Occasionally it occurs during infancy or early childhood: while still in his cradle Hercules kills two serpents sent by Hera to kill him, and the boy Odysseus proves himself by defeating a wild boar. The initiation does not necessarily occur in childhood, of course; David is already grown to manhood when he kills Goliath. And sometimes this rite of passage takes the form of a divine sign: the words from heaven on the occasion of Jesus' baptism, the words of God in the burning bush. Whenever and wherever it occurs, however, this initiation tells us of the presence of that very special being, the hero.

The confrontation with giants, monsters, and wild beasts symbolizes another aspect of this process of initiation. Here the hero learns to control the fantasies of childhood, those fantasies in which all adults are giants and all memories exaggerated. The childhood initiation is but the first of many rites of passage that the hero must endure. It resembles the kind of rebirth expressed in circumcision rituals, which are intended to deliver the child dramatically from the world of the nursery to that of adult responsibility.

Having learned through initiation of his heroic nature, the hero frequently withdraws for a period of inner trial and self-confrontation. Interestingly enough, he frequently retreats during this period to a womblike place reminiscent of his place of birth and symbolic of his rebirth as a mature adult. Mohammed, for instance, hides in a cave; Jesus goes into the wilderness for forty days; Moses spends a like amount of time on Mount Sinai; and the Buddha meditates for weeks under the bo tree.

The Ojibwa Indians tell of such a withdrawal in the story of Wunzh, whose vigil in the woods is a prototype for the vigil of Hiawatha in Longfellow's poem. Wunzh, the oldest child of a devout but poor Indian family, reaches the age when Ojibwa youths go through *Keiguishimowin*, a ritual fast to discover their guardian spirits. In the spring Wunzh's family builds him a little hut in a lonely spot where he begins his fast in solitude. During the first days of his vigil the boy walks through the woods, his mind filled with pleasant dreams. He seeks to discover how plants grow without man's help and why some are good to eat and others not.

When Wunzh becomes too weak from fasting to walk further, he retires to his hut, where he awaits the dreams that he hopes will help his family in their struggle for existence. He begs the Great Spirit for advice on how to obtain food for his family and his tribe by some means other than hunting and fishing. Finally, weak and faint, Wunzh repairs to his bed, where he has a vision in which a fine young man descends from the sky and walks toward him. This man is dressed in various shades of yellow and green and has feathers on his head. "I come from the Great Spirit in answer to your prayers," he tells

Wunzh. "I will teach you what to do to help your people." He then informs the boy that the lad will have to wrestle with him in order to make his wishes come true. In spite of his weakness, Wunzh fights until he nearly collapses. "Enough," says the smiling visitor as he ascends into the air. "I will come again tomorrow."

The next day the visitor returns and the wrestling is resumed. Although he has even less strength than before, Wunzh feels that his spirit has grown—and again he fights until he is on the brink of exhaustion. "Enough," the visitor says at last. "I shall return tomorrow."

On the third day the youth finds himself still weaker in body but proportionately stronger mentally—and this time the stranger concedes defeat, enters the hut, and begins instructing the youth. "Because you have wrestled so well," he says, "the Great Spirit will grant your desires. Tomorrow your father will offer you food because it will be your seventh day of fasting. Do not eat until I have wrestled with you one more time, however. And when you have defeated me, strip me of my clothes and bury me in the earth, which you will prepare by clearing a spot in the weeds and making the ground soft. Then come at regular intervals to remove the weeds from my grave and to cover me with fresh earth. If you do as I say you will learn something of great benefit to your fellow creatures, something you may then teach them."

Wunzh's father does bring food, which he urges the boy to eat. The boy, for his part, begs his father to leave him until sundown, which the old man dutifully does. Then, at the same hour as on each of the previous days, the stranger comes from the sky. The wrestling recommences and the boy, now endowed with superhuman spiritual strength, easily prevails. He throws his opponent to the ground, strips him, and buries him according to instructions. Wunzh then returns to his father's lodge to eat the food that has been prepared for him.

Throughout the spring he visits the grave of his mysterious visitor and tends it carefully—and soon he sees the green plumes of the sky visitor's headgear pushing through the ground. Weeks pass. Then in the late summer Wunzh asks his father to follow him to the place where he fasted. The nearby grave is now dominated by a magnificent plant with yellow tassels falling like tresses from its crown. "This is my sky friend," the boy declares. "He is Mondawmin, the grain spirit, the friend of us all. Now we do not have to depend only on hunting and fishing for food. If we follow the ways of this spirit we will have food from the ground itself. The Great Spirit has rewarded me for my fast."

In his period of withdrawal, Jesus went into the wilderness, where he was tempted by Satan; at left, one of the temptations as it appears in a thirteenth-century French psalter.

From this story several elements of the heroic monomyth emerge. The wrestling matches, the instructions from the spirit world, and the resurrection of the divine visitor all remind us of the Bear Man story, another instance in which death led to new life. As we have seen, resurrection stories are usually closely related to the planting of crops. In this story, as in the Bear Man story, we also find the shamanistic aspects so important to the hero myth. The hero, like the shaman, is one who learns unknown practices from unknown powers—and then uses them to benefit mankind. It is this shamanic quality that most informs the withdrawal period of the hero's life, for it is this period that stresses the importance of food for the spirit as opposed to food for the body. When the hero withdraws into the wilderness—or the mountains, or a cave—he withdraws into himself in preparation for a second birth, emerging from solitude with a divinity he has acquired there. This often involves physical as well as mental suffering, both preparation for the withdrawal into death that awaits the hero later in life. In most withdrawal stories, the hero is severely tempted by demons of the sensual or material world, temptation representing those things that prevent human beings from experiencing the inner self, an experience necessary for the attainment of psychic wholeness.

When he leaves the wilderness, the hero is fully prepared for the quest or trials of his adult life, for during his seclusion he has learned the magic he will need to break out of the tragic cycle of life. For centuries one of the most popular of the world's quest stories has been that of the Holy Grail, the cup used by Jesus at the Last Supper. It is said that Joseph of Arimathea carried the sacred cup to England along with the spear used to pierce Jesus' side during the Crucifixion. In time the care of these relics passed to Joseph's descendants, who were instructed to maintain absolute purity of thought, word, and deed. Pilgrims came from all corners of the world to see the Grail and the lance—until one of the guardians forgot his vow of purity long enough to look lustfully upon a girl who had come to see the relics. Instantly the holy lance pierced him, causing a wound which would not heal, and the Grail disappeared.

The great magician Merlin sent a message to King Arthur, asking him to head a search for the Grail, and Sir Gawain, who had delivered Merlin's message, vowed that he would leave immediately in search of the holy relic. Most of the other knights made the same vow, and Arthur bemoaned the breaking up of his society of knights.

At this point the story focuses upon the exploits of two of the knights, Percival and Gawain. One day Percival comes upon a man who is fishing in a great lake. Although pallid and despondent, this stranger is finely dressed, and Percival asks him if he knows of any place where he might take shelter for the night. The fisherman directs Percival to a nearby castle, which the knight reaches only with difficulty but where he is lavishly received. He enters a richly decorated and well-lit hall where four hundred melancholy knights sit at small tables. Their faces brighten when Percival enters the room, as if to indicate that he is an expected and most welcome guest. The lord of the castle, also wan and weak, sits near the fire. After seating his guest alongside him, the pale lord tells Percival that he has been expected for a long time. He then gives the baffled knight a fine sword.

At this point a servant enters carrying a blood-stained lance in silent procession around the room. Percival wonders about the meaning of this macabre display, but out of politeness he does not question his host about it. Several beautiful maidens now enter the room followed by a queenly woman who carries a radiant cup. All around him Percival hears voices whisper "the Holy Grail!" but again politeness prevents him from questioning his host. After the maidens have left,

the pages offer their masters drink, which flows in apparently infinite quantity from the sacred cup. When the feast ends the lord of the castle is helped to his feet by two servants. He stares wistfully at Percival, heaves a great sigh, and leaves the room. Servants then lead the young knight to his room, in which there is a tapestry depicting a battle. It shows the lord of the castle being wounded by a weapon identical to the one carried around the banquet hall. Percival is by now burning with curiosity, but he decides to put off his questions until morning.

At daybreak Percival wakes to find his clothes by his bed but no servants to help him dress. All doors in the castle are locked except those leading to the outside courtyard, where his horse stands saddled and waiting. As he crosses the drawbridge a voice calls out to him from the ramparts, "Thou art cursed by God. Chosen to do a great work, thou hast not done it. Follow thy path to hell."

Sir Gawain fares rather differently. He too finds his way to the castle. During the banquet held upon his arrival a procession of beautiful maidens—one wearing a crown—enters the hall carrying a spear, a salver, and a magnificent cup. The spear is then laid before the lord of the castle with the salver under it—and as Gawain and the others watch transfixed, the spear sheds three drops of blood into the salver. A cup is then placed before Gawain's host. From it the old man extracts a piece of bread, which he eats. Gawain can contain himself no longer: "In the name of God," he cries, "tell me, my host, what all this means!" As he speaks all present spring from their seats and begin rejoicing. "Sir Gawain," the old man says, "what you behold is a miracle of God and as you have asked I may not hide from you the truth. You see before you the Holy Grail. By achieving this difficult quest you have won the praise of all mankind and brought much gladness, for many are now freed from sorrow."

In this story Percival represents the archetype of the hero who refuses the call. He stands for those of us who would prefer not to ask who we are, who put off the necessary confrontation and communion with the mythic reality within and around us. Gawain, on the other hand, is the true seeker. On the surface, of course, he is specifically a Christian hero, and by saving the king and his kingdom he imitates Christ. Christian symbolism is evident, too, in the assistance of the crowned maiden—the interceding virgin—and in the ritual meal of bread and blood. But the Grail legend can also be traced back to fertility rites as ancient as those of Attis and Cybele—the spear being a male symbol, the cup a female symbol, and the land of the king a sterile one whose infertility the hero must overcome. Thus Gawain is but another manifestation of the world hero as quester-saviour.

In a sense, of course, the quest myth is the *only* hero myth, for the hero's entire life, from birth to apotheosis, can be seen as a quest for wholeness. However, there does come a time during the hero's life when he finds himself totally committed to a particular search or trial within this larger quest. Gawain's ultimate goal is union with his God, but his particular goal is to locate the Holy Grail. The search, as we have seen, is an expression of every human being's need to prove

The hero's quest or trial is related in tales from two widely separated mythic cultures: above, Theseus slays the Minotaur (left) and Jason reaches for the Golden Fleece (right)—both depicted on classic-period Greek vases; below, damsels carry the Holy Grail before Percival in a scene from the renowned Arthurian legend.

himself. Having established his origins and discovered the divine destiny within himself, the hero now acts according to that destiny. The quest, then, is symbolic of the move from the inner sufferings of adolescence to the active pursuits of the prime of life. If birth, initiation, and withdrawal are the springtime of the hero's life, this is the summer.

For some heroes the quest stage involves being pushed to the very edge of human experience. Thus Hercules travels to the borders of the universe and Theseus pursues the Minotaur into the depths of the Labyrinth. Similarly, Jesus and Dionysus both reach beyond the boundaries of human power to perform miracles designed to lead humans to fuller realization of themselves.

Whatever form it takes, the particular quest always reflects the universal one—which is for eternal life through a confrontation with death. In pursuit of this goal the hero must descend into the underworld, a journey that represents a second withdrawal from life in preparation for a rebirth that will be both actual and symbolic. An ancient Eddic lay called the *Havamal* tells of the god Odin, who dies by hanging on the world tree Yggdrasill:

> I know I hung
> for nine days
> on the wind-driven tree . . .
> I was not given bread
> or the drinking horn.
> Downward I peered
> and grasped the runes,
> howling I grasped them,
> and fell away from there.

The frequent association of a tree with the death of a hero is significant, for these trees are all held to have roots in the depths of the unknown. The tree is also a symbol of life and fertility, and therefore even in death the hero is cradled by the promise of renewed life. Through his death he teaches us something of the positive aspects of dying, of the rebirth of the spirit. Thus Odin from his tree looks downward toward the unknown roots and grasps the runes, or mysteries. Here again, as in the withdrawal stage, the hero can be compared to the shaman. Odin's runes are the holy words and rites of the shaman, of the one who provides the necessary link between human beings and the other world. Death is the gateway to that world, and the shaman, in a trance induced by dancing, chanting, drugs, or some other means, can pass through that gateway and intercede for unheroic, ordinary men.

Having passed through the gates of death, the hero, like the shaman, endeavors to overpower death from within by descending as far as he can into the other kingdom. One of the oldest versions of this story is the Babylonian-Sumerian myth of Inanna, who journeys to the underworld to retrieve her lover, Tammuz. Dressed in her best clothes and jewels Inanna prepares to visit the Land of No Return, which is presided over by her sister, Ereshkigal, who is also her sworn enemy. Realizing that her sister will almost certainly attempt to kill her, Inanna tells her messenger, Ninshubur, that if she fails to return in three days he is to go to the god Enlil and beg for assistance. In the event that Enlil should refuse, Ninshubur is to make the same plea to Nanna, the moon-god. And should Nanna refuse, Ninshubur is to seek out Enki, the god of wisdom.

Inanna now enters the confines of the underworld and advances toward Ereshkigal's temple. There she is met by a gatekeeper who leads Inanna through seven gates, at each of which she is stripped of part of her clothes or jewels. At last she passes through the final gate, where she is forced to appear naked before her sister and the Anunnaki, the seven judges of the underworld. The judges pronounce the curse of death and Inanna is hanged from a stake.

Three days and nights pass and on the fourth day Ninshubur follows the instructions given him by his mistress. Enlil and Nanna both refuse to help; only Enki consents. He creates two sexless creatures, supplies them with the "food of life" and the "water of life," and tells them to enter Ereshkigal's land and sprinkle the food and water sixty times on the corpse of Inanna. This is done, the goddess revives, and she returns to the upper world accompanied by the shades of the dead.

In this phase, the descent to the underworld, the world hero once again serves as humanity's scapegoat by confronting, face-to-face, that which man most fears. Often this descent is coupled with the idea that by descending into the earth the hero returns to his natural mother. This is the stage of the germinating seed, and here many heroes—Bear Man, Attis, Osiris, and Mondawmin among them—must spend time before being born again in the spring.

These interpretations point to the psychological function of the descent motif in mythology. The underworld journey is the "night journey," the voyage into the "dark night of the soul." It is the ultimate meditation, the exploration of lives already lived. As the archetype of the self, the world hero actually supplants the ruler of the dark world, the world of the collective unconscious. In Egyptian mythology, for instance, Osiris becomes king of the underworld. And in Babylonian legend Inanna, "goddess of light and love and life," enters the nether world to confront her other self in the form of her sister Ereshkigal, "goddess of darkness, gloom, and death." This sense of recognizing and bringing together the opposing aspects of the self —good and evil, flesh and spirit, light and dark, *yin* and *yang*—is the very essence of the underworld theme.

Osiris is said to have given the Egyptians their first laws, and, through his sister-wife, Isis, to have introduced the cultivation of wheat and barley. As a result he was widely worshiped in ancient Egypt. But according to a classic tale Osiris had a jealous brother, Set, who plotted against him. Set tricked the god-king into entering a coffer, which he and his henchmen then nailed shut and threw into the Nile. Isis, dressed thereafter in mourning, wandered the earth in search of her husband's body, which had floated out to sea and landed at Byblos in what is now Lebanon. Immediately a tree sprang up,

The death of a hero has never been more poignantly recounted than in the New Testament description of the Crucifixion of Jesus; above, the dramatic moment as captured in a thirteenth-century French psalter.

enveloping the coffer in its trunk. The king of Byblos then cut the tree down and used the trunk as a pillar in his palace. When Isis learned of this she traveled to Byblos, where she asked for and promptly received the pillar. After extracting the coffer, she wrapped the pillar in a fine cloth and presented it to the king, who placed it in the Temple of Isis in Byblos. The mourning Isis then took the coffer by boat back to Egypt.

One day Isis left the coffer and went to visit her son Horus, who had been conceived miraculously when Isis, taking the form of a hawk, flew over the corpse of her murdered husband. While she was gone, evil Set came upon the coffer. He recognized the body, which he cut into fourteen pieces and scattered across the terrain. Isis returned, discovered her loss, and began a protracted search for the pieces. In time she found everything but the genitals. Again she lamented her dead husband, and this time the sun-god Ra took pity on her and sent the god Anubis, who pieced together the body, wrapped it in linen, and performed funeral rites over it. Isis then fanned the body with her wings, and miraculously Osiris revived.

The Osiris story tells us a great deal about the meaning of the resurrection or rebirth motif in general. In the Egyptian story Set is the personification of evil, yet he also plays the role of the sower of seed (represented here by Osiris' body and elsewhere by the dismembered bodies of other heroes). Without Set the resurrection would not have occurred, and thus in the purely ritualistic sense his function is the same as that of Wunzh in the Mondawmin story, which also focuses upon the death and rebirth of a grain deity.

Following his death but before his glorious resurrection and ascent into heaven, Jesus — according to the creed of the Christian faith — descended to the underworld; the horrifying mouth of hell is shown at left, below, in a twelfth-century English psalter. The Egyptian god Osiris (left) had one of mythology's most remarkable rebirths. In his apotheosis Mohammed reached the Seventh Heaven; at right, the prophet appears as a flame ascending Islam's seven-tiered celestial abode.

In the events of Osiris' life the ancient Egyptians saw a promise of eternal life for themselves after death. As Osiris turned dead seeds into plants, so he himself was transformed from dead to living god. Through him they could find life in death—and until the advent of Islam Egyptians believed that to follow in Osiris' path they needed only to have their dead bodies molded and mummified as the god's had been. At funerary rites the deceased was referred to as "Osiris so and so" and professional female mourners sang Isis' lament over the corpse. In one Egyptian text these words are found: "As Osiris lives, so shall this man live; as Osiris did not die, he shall not die; as Osiris is not destroyed, he shall not be destroyed."

The pattern of rebirth and resurrection is universal. In all its manifestations the hero moves from a state of nonlife to one of extraordinary life, and in this final stage there is a repetition of the miraculous birth. Death is definitively defeated—often with its own inadvertent help—and the cycle of nature is completed by the hero's return to life. Psychologically this is the culmination of the process of self-realization or individuation that produces the whole man. The monsters and gargoyles of the past have been defeated and the individual emerges now in his new form, having fully explored the depths of the collective being. As Joseph Campbell has remarked, the hero "has died as a modern man, but as eternal man—perfected, unspecific, universal man—he has been reborn."

The apostles Matthew and Luke tell this story of the ascension of Jesus into heaven:

Then the eleven disciples went away into Galilee, into a mountain where Jesus had appointed them. And when they saw him they worshipped him: but some doubted. And Jesus came and spake unto them, saying, All power is given unto me in heaven and in earth. Go ye therefore, and teach all nations, baptizing them in the name of the Father, and of the Son, and of the Holy Ghost: teaching them to observe all things whatsoever I have commanded you: and, lo, I am with you always, even unto the end of the world. (Matthew 28:16–20)

And he led them out as far as to Bethany, and he lifted up his hands, and blessed them. And it came to pass, while he blessed them, he was parted from them, and carried up into heaven. And they worshipped him, and returned to Jerusalem with great joy: and were continually in the temple, praising and blessing God. (Luke 24:50–53)

Forty days after Easter, as the sun approaches mid-heaven following the vernal equinox, Christians celebrate this event with the Feast of the Assumption. Jesus is far from being the only heroic figure assumed into heaven, however. The list is a long one, and it includes the Persian Mithras, Dionysus, the prophet Elijah, Saint Francis of Assisi—and, in a substantially later addition to Christ's ascension, the Virgin Mary, who is said to have been physically assumed into heaven to reign there with her martyred son. Moreover, ascension is but one form of apotheosis with the unknown. According to ancient Judaic legend, the soul of Moses was taken by God with a kiss and the soul of Abraham was carried to heaven by the angel Michael. Elsewhere, apotheosis is represented by miracles attending a hero's funeral. The Buddha's funeral pyre reportedly ignited spontaneously, for instance, and when it had burned completely he was released from his corporeal self to achieve nirvana, oneness with all things.

The myth of apotheosis is the logical conclusion of the hero's adventures. Through it he is given permanent status in a universal context; his divinity is recognized in heaven. Having been miraculously conceived out of the void, he now returns to the void. Human beings, seeking to pattern their lives on those of their heroes, are led in the direction of the universally valid human norms, freedom and unity. To ascend to heaven is to achieve freedom from fear and the limitations of time. He who follows the hero gains a true self through the loss of the illusion of personal and local self. The beginning of the path to psychic wholeness, then, is the recognition that the hero's voyage is potentially the voyage of Everyman.

Gods of the North

The great myth cycles of Celtic civilization were not officially transcribed until the Middle Ages—when verse epics like *The Mabinogion*, source of the earliest version of the legend of King Arthur, were composed. But those cycles existed in oral form from pre-Christian times. Indeed, as early as the fourth century B.C. the Celts were recognized as an important cultural and military presence on the Continent, and their influence was felt from Asia Minor to the British Isles. Celtic tribesmen sacked Rome in 390 B.C. and plundered Delphi a century later, but nowhere was their impact greater than in Ireland, where they ruled without serious opposition for a thousand years. There the Celtic tongue was spoken, and there the heroic tales that are the central feature of Celtic mythology were set down. The men who compiled those myth cycles were, for the most part, Christian monks, and as a result the ancient legends of the insular Celts are tainted with biblical moralizing. On the Continent itself Celtic legends lost their mythic purity at a far earlier date, gradually melding with the religious beliefs of the conquering Romans who swept into Gaul in the first century B.C. "Of the gods they worship Mercury most of all," wrote Julius Caesar in his *Commentaries on the Gallic War*. His observation was only half correct, for although Mercury did rank above all adopted deities he ranked below the ancient Celtic pantheon headed by Cernunnos, the horned god. This subordination of foreign gods is evident in the Gallo-Roman bas-relief above, which shows the cross-legged Cernunnos seated between Apollo (left) and Mercury, both clearly attendant upon the supreme Celtic deity.

Indisputably the most popular of Gallo-Roman gods, Mercury was revered above Mars, Apollo, and mighty Jupiter by the Celts. The bronze statuette at near left shows this immensely popular adopted god with his sacred animals, the goat, cock, and tortoise. Interestingly enough, this process of adoption worked both ways in occupied Gaul, with Caesar's cavalry recognizing the Celtic goddess Epona, seen at far left, as protectoress of their stables. Although each Celtic tribe honored its own pantheon, certain gods were shared by all. These included the chieftain-deity Cernunnos, who presided over a host of zoomorphic subdeities in both insular and Continental iconography. Perhaps the most celebrated of all Celtic artifacts is the silver-plated copper cauldron below, discovered in a peat bog near Gundestrop, Denmark, in 1891. Its outer surface is banded with images of local deities and its inner surface is embellished with scenes from familiar myths. One of these inner panels (shown at lower left) is devoted exclusively to Cernunnos.

Scandinavian mythology, born on the western shores of the Baltic Sea in the middle of the second millennium B.C., had little impact upon the cultural evolution of the rest of Europe for the next two thousand years. With the rise of the Vikings in the ninth century A.D., however, all this was to change; over the next two hundred years these fearsome warriors were to leave their mark from Greenland to the Mediterranean and from the Volga to the coast of North America. And by the time Viking depredations ended, the principal victims of those raids, the Anglo-Saxons, had renamed three days of the week to honor the three principal deities of the Teutonic pantheon: Woden, Thor, and Frija. Odin, as the Viking Jupiter was also called, ruled in Valhalla, where he entertained fallen warriors at a perpetual "feast beyond the grave." Although representations of Odin are rare, he does appear on the so-called Gotland Memorial Stone, opposite. On the bottom register of that stele—beneath a battle scene and a depiction of a boatload of souls bound for Valhalla—archers defend a closed compound against a lone warrior supported by eagles. That solitary figure can only be Odin, whom Scandinavian legend credits with having transformed himself into an eagle in order to win the "mead of inspiration" for men. Odin and his fellow deities dwelt in Asgard, a walled city whose chief defender was the red-haired thunder-god, Thor. The better to perform this task Thor wore a special belt that gave him superhuman strength and gloves that enabled him to crush rocks. As the statuette at right indicates, this most beloved of Teutonic gods also carried a mighty war hammer, Mjolnir, with which he slew the monsters and giants that assailed Asgard. Within Valhalla itself the valiant dead were attended by warrior-maidens known as valkyries, ethereally beautiful females who wandered the field of battle and summoned slain heroes to Valhalla with blasts from a ram's horn. The silver and bronze amulets below are thought to depict these guardians of the final rest—and one of them does indeed carry a ram's horn before her.

Viking warriors spent much of their lives at sea, crossing and recrossing the icy waters of the Baltic, the North Sea, and the northern Atlantic in their vividly colored "long ships." It is hardly surprising, therefore, that a number of Viking chieftains chose to spend eternity at the helm of a dragon-prowed corsair. In some instances this meant putting a torch to the deceased commander's pitch-soaked vessel and then setting the flaming craft adrift. More often, however, it involved interring the entire ship on dry land. One of the most famous of these Viking ship burials was unearthed at Oseberg, Norway, in 1904. The dragon's head at near right, one of five recovered at the site, was erected above the mound specifically to scare off would-be graverobbers. (Their curse undimmed by the passage of time, these malignant spirits so terrified the native workmen who discovered them at the turn of the century that they deliberately desecrated several heads to escape the dragons' spell.) As famous —and far more sumptuous—is the treasure from Sutton Hoo, a burial site in Suffolk, England. It includes the iron helmet opposite, an exquisite example of Viking handiwork overlaid with bronze and embellished with silver, gilt, and garnets. The workmanship is almost certainly Swedish, yet the grave itself is plainly that of a seventh-century East Anglian prince—a circumstance that only serves to underscore how strong the cultural bond between the two regions was at the time. The highly stylized eagle above, also recovered at Sutton Hoo, is Odin's familiar totem, executed this time in iron, bronze, gold leaf, and inlaid glass. Once part of an enormous, circular ceremonial shield, this familiar Teutonic emblem served as a reminder that Odin often assumed feathered form to sit atop the world tree.

The peoples of Scandinavia were not converted to Christianity until the tenth and eleventh centuries, but the influence of the Church was felt from a much earlier time. The seventh-century treasure of Sutton Hoo contains both Christian and pagan objects, and elements from both traditions are present in the relief work on the Frank's Casket, a small whalebone chest carved in Northumbria during the same period. This fusion of mythologies is especially evident on the front panel (above), which pairs a tale from Norse legend with a biblical event. At left, the princess Bodvild presents her baseborn husband, Weland, with a son; at right, the Adoration of the Magi. The so-called stave churches of Norway and Sweden retained their pagan architectural details—such as dragon-headed ridgepoles and ancient cult totems—long after those buildings were converted to Christian worship. The crudely carved visage at near right, thought to be the one-eyed Odin, still graces one such church. (The principal means of sacrifice to Odin was garroting, which would explain the lolling tongue and bulging eye of the statue.) At far right, a pagan archway frames the altar of a twelfth-century stave church in Setesdal, Norway. Scenes from the life of Sigurd, hero of the Scandinavian legend cycle known as the *Völsunga Saga*, are carved in high relief on either side of the archway. They show Sigurd, a mortal descendant of mighty Odin, slaying the dragon Fafnir (top, right) and roasting its heart (top, left). The great mythic tales of the North were preserved in oral form until the thirteenth century, when an Icelandic poet named Snorri Sturluson compiled the *Prose Edda*, a handbook of the ancient sagas of the Scandinavian peoples. Until Snorri's time the only written records kept by the Vikings were cryptic runestones such as the one at top right. The messages inscribed on these stones could be read by almost no one, but that may not have mattered: it was thought that the runes themselves had mystical powers.

5

The Mythmakers

WHEN AN AMERICAN INDIAN SHAMAN enters the dwelling of a sick person, he brings a great deal of paraphernalia. There is the small mat on which he will sit for hours alongside the patient; there is the drumrattle made of the skin of a doe's ears with which he will keep time as he dances around the sickbed. There are also the beads he will wear, the bird feathers he will scatter, and the pipe containing herbal tobacco he will smoke. But the most potent medicine he brings is the Word, which will emerge in the form of a trance-induced song.

Holding a shell over a man with a diseased leg, an old Chippewa shaman chants, "You will live again, you will walk. Through my holy power and this shell you shall walk again." Later the shaman sings to the patient's spirit, the spirit for which he is contending with the dark forces in the other world:

> O Spirit of Morning
> O Spirit of Dusk
> O Spirit of Rain
> O Spirit of Wind,
> Darkness is here.
> I offer smoke to you
> O Great Spirit
> Make new my leg
> Renew my body,
> Deny your spell.
> You who made Morning
> From stars
> And Dusk from Raven,
> You who made Rain
> From your sweat and
> Wind from your movement,
> Renew my body
> Deny your spell.

The shaman who sings such a song may be a Navajo or an Eskimo, Tartar or Siberian. When asked to describe his trance and his song, he will say that he has been to the other world, that he was entered the spirit of the sick person and there produced something that can translate universally as the Word. He may also say that his song was a

Indians of the American Southwest have inherited a rich mythic tradition with a lively cast of religious spirits called kachinas. In secret ceremonies held in circular, semisubterranean chambers initiated men assumed the personalities of these kachinas by donning fantastic costumes. Opposite, the culture's critical cloud spirit is vividly represented by a Hopi kachina doll.

materialization of that Word, the very substance of life and reality—an expression of that ultimate creative force that informs all things. Not illogically, myths of creation tend to spring from these shamanic trance songs, for the reality of the Word is what we defined earlier as myth in its most basic form—"In the beginning was the Word." In a very real sense, then, the shamanic trance—and resultant song—comes closer than any other ritual activity to replicating, in miniature, the mythmaking process. For one thing, it begins to tell us who first put the Word into words.

The original—and ultimate—mythmaker is of course the psyche, from whence are drawn the motifs of the evil brother, the descent to the underworld, and the virgin birth. But the articulator of myth, the one who gives voice to the human soul through language, is the shaman and his descendant the wild-eyed poet, the "singer of tales."

When a Mazatec Indian shaman from Mexico eats a certain mushroom he becomes possessed by a force outside himself. He then sings a song that is both healing incantation and powerful poetry:

> The one who speaks to the mountain I am,
> The one who speaks to the Father I am,
> The one who speaks to the Mother.
> I speak the soul of day,
> I speak the mountain river,
> I speak the fullness of harvest.
> I speak the terror of day,
> The path of dawn.

The same two elements are present in these lines, written by the English romantic poet William Wordsworth:

> Oft in these moments such a holy calm
> Did overspread my soul, that I forgot
> That I had bodily eyes, and what I saw
> Appear'd like something in myself, a dream,
> A prospect in my mind.

One summer day in 1791 Wordsworth's friend Samuel Taylor Coleridge underwent an experience that provides us with even deeper insight into the shamanic nature of the poetic act. Coleridge, who was ill, had taken a prescribed dose of opium and had fallen asleep while reading the following passage in an old book: "Here the Khan Kubla commanded a palace to be built, and a stately garden thereunto. And thus ten miles of fertile ground were inclosed with a wall." During his sleep, the poet formed the distinct impression that he was composing some three hundred lines of poetry. All the images rose up before him "as *things*, with a parallel production of the correspondent expressions, without any sensation or consciousness of effort." As soon as he awoke Coleridge began writing out lines of poetry. The arrival of an unexpected visitor interrupted his labors before the poem was finished, however, and when Coleridge returned to his task sometime later he discovered that the spell had been broken, the vision lost. The resultant fragment is *Kubla Khan*—a poem which, with its descent "to a sun-

The mythology of the North-west Coast Indians, whose lands stretched from the Puget Sound to the Alaskan panhandle, inspired a startlingly vivid art best known for its awesome totem poles. The small, beautifully crafted objects opposite include Tlingit (top) and Kitskan charms at near right and a Kwakiutl wooden bear mask at far right.

less sea," its "woman wailing for her demon-lover," and its "ancestral voices," has all the markings of a shamanic song. This is most evident in the last section:

> A damsel with a dulcimer
> In a vision once I saw:
> It was an Abyssinian maid,
> And on her dulcimer she played,
> Singing of Mount Abora.
> Could I revive within me
> Her symphony and song,
> To such delight 'twould win me,
> That with music loud and long,
> I would build that dome in air,
> That sunny dome! those caves of ice!
> And all who hear should see them there,
> And all should cry, Beware! Beware!
> His flashing eyes, his floating hair!
> Weave a circle around him thrice,
> And close your eyes with holy dread,
> For he on honey-dew hath fed,
> And drunk the milk of Paradise.

Coleridge, the modern poet in the act of creation, had experienced a vision not unlike that of his archetypal ancestor, the shaman; both had been touched by the Word.

As these examples, ancient and modern, of the mythmaking process indicate, neither the shaman nor the poet achieves the moment of creative ecstasy without an ordeal of preparation. Take the case of the Eskimo shaman Igjugarjuk, who told a researcher early in this century that when he was being initiated into shamanism he lived in solitude for thirty days, eating nothing, and that the cold and the hunger caused him to "die a little" each day. Only then did a guardian spirit appear to him and give him the power to see visions of the unknown. In

119

truth, the preparation and the shamanic cure are so demanding as to make many shamans into mythic heroes themselves. In the following story, told by the Tlingit Indians, the boy hero is clearly derived from the tradition of the shaman, learning his trade and making the great journey.

Two boys, the older of whom is a chief's son, regularly play a game that involves making as many arrows as possible. One fine night when the moon is full they take their arrows to a beautiful grassy knoll behind the village. On their way there the younger boy says to his friend, "Look at the moon. Don't you think it looks like my mother's lip-piece?" The older boy, clearly upset by this sacrilegious talk, warns the other against making fun of the moon—but he has scarcely finished when the night becomes completely dark and the two boys are surrounded by a luminous ring. When the ring disappears, the younger boy does too. "My goodness," the chief's son declares, "the strange ring must have been the moon. The moon has taken away my friend."

Left alone, the boy begins to cry. To console himself he tries the bows that he and his friend brought with them. All of the bows break except for one made of a very hard wood. With it the boy decides to shoot at the star next to the moon. He does so, and then sits down to watch the effect. Before long the star darkens. Encouraged, he shoots his entire pile of arrows at the dim star. The arrows do not appear to fall back to earth, but after a while the boy notices a chain of arrows hanging next to him.

Tired and sad, the boy now falls asleep. When he awakens hours later he discovers that the arrow chain has become a ladder to the sky. He decides to climb the ladder, but before doing so he ties various kinds of plants to the knot in his hair. All day he climbs the ladder, and at nightfall he camps upon it. In the morning he eats berries that have appeared on the salmonberry bush in his hair, and he immediately feels mysteriously stronger. At noontime he eats berries from the huckleberry bush in his hair; the following morning, blackberries.

At the top of the ladder the boy finds a lake, beside which he rests on some moss. While he is asleep he thinks he feels someone shake him and he hears a voice saying, "Arise, I have come for you." Peering through partially closed eyes he sees a beautiful young girl approaching him. She is dressed in clothes made of animal skins and leggings decorated with the quills of porcupines. The chief's son follows this girl to a little house where he is greeted by an old woman who asks, "Why have you traveled way up here, my grandson?" The boy explains that he has come in search of his friend. "Oh, he is next door in the moon's house," the old woman says. "I hear him crying all the time." Then the woman gives the boy a spruce cone, part of a devil's club plant, a rose bush, and a piece of whetstone and sends him to find his friend.

When he arrives at the moon's house the boy hears his friend screaming. Discovering that his friend is being held captive near the smoke hole in the roof, the chief's son climbs down the hole and rescues his playmate. He then takes the spruce cone given to him by the old woman, places it in the chimney hole where his friend has been, and commands it to imitate the boy's cries of pain.

120

Soon after the pair escape, however, the cone drops to the floor—and the moon begins to pursue the boys. Seeing that they are in danger of being overtaken, the older boy drops the devil's club behind him. A dense patch of devil's club sprouts on the spot, and it briefly slows down the moon. (Later the youth repeats the same move with the rose bush.) As the moon draws close for the third time the boy drops the whetstone. It becomes a cliff over which the moon cannot climb. When they finally reach the old woman's house the boys embrace joyfully.

After feeding the boys the old woman sends them to the top of the ladder, where she instructs them to lie down with closed eyes and think of nothing but the grassy hill at the bottom of the ladder. The boys do as they were told, and soon they are lying at the foot of the ladder on the hill behind their village.

All of the shamanic elements are found in this story: the two sets of paraphernalia, the voyage to the other world, the ritual actions, the retrieval of a lost person, the instruction by guardian spirits, and the miraculous return from apparent death. The shaman literally lived the mythic experience, so that it is altogether logical that his ritual songs became the basis for stories such as the one told above. Indeed, to the American Indians the shaman *was* a living mythic character, and in their stories about him he could take many forms—could become even the culture hero himself.

In ancient times the poet, too, sometimes underwent a shamanlike ordeal. In Ireland, for example, the *seanchan*, or master poet, was required to pass through seven stages of wisdom in a difficult twelve-year training period. This training included a period of ritual solitude, of waiting for the spirit that characterizes the shamanic process. And when the modern Irish poet W. B. Yeats wrote his famous poem, *The Lake Isle of Innisfree*, he conveyed something of the poet's longing for the kind of mythmaking vision that the ancient bard awaited in his solitude:

> I will arise and go now, and go to Innisfree,
> And a small cabin build there, of clay and wattles made:
> Nine bean-rows will I have there, a hive for the honeybee,
> And live alone in the bee-loud glade.
>
> And I shall have some peace there, for peace comes dropping slow,
> Dropping from the veils of morning to where the cricket sings;
> There midnight's all a glimmer, and noon a purple glow,
> And evening full of the linnet's wings.
>
> I will arise and go now, for always night and day
> I hear lake water lapping with low sounds by the shore;
> While I stand on the roadway, or on the pavements grey,
> I hear it in the deep heart's core.

The poet of old was a medium between man and his gods. He was a seer, and as such he shared with the shaman and the mythic hero the terror and ecstasy of the mythic experience. Ideally, then, the poet also follows the heroic path: he is "born, not made," and although he must go through the agony of his own life he is reborn in his verses as eternal man whose universal language is myth. Believing this to be so, ancient man held the poet in awe and greatly honored him. It was to Homer and Hesiod, then, that the ancient Greeks looked for the revelation of the mysteries of gods and heroes. It was they who were able to break through the boundaries of our human existence and make the Word speak in words, and given this holy aspect poets themselves sometimes became the subjects of mythic stories. In the Middle Ages, for instance, Vergil was mythologized into a magician-sorcerer, a trickster figure who played games with the dead and could haunt the living. But the most mythic of all is the unknown author of the following lines:

> Remember me later on,
> whenever someone of the men of earth
> finds himself here, a stranger
> who has suffered a lot,
> and he says to you,
> "O girls,
> who is the sweetest man
> that comes here
> with his songs for you,
> who is it
> that pleases you the most?"
> Then, all together, answer him:
> "A blind man,
> he lives in rocky Chios,
> and all his songs will still be the best
> at the end of time."

Homer, like Tiresias and Oedipus, was blind, but like them he had insight into matters both human and divine. If there really *was* such a man, we have his self-portrait in the *Odyssey:*

> And a herald came near, leading the trusty singer
> Demodocos, honored by the people. And he set him
> In the midst of the diners, propped against a tall pillar.
> Then Odysseus of many devices addressed the herald
> When he had cut some off the back—but more was left on it—
> Of a shining-tusked boar; and swelling fat was about it.
> "Herald, take this portion over to Demodocos,
> So he may eat, and I will embrace him, grieved as I am,
> For among all the men on the earth singers are sharers
> In honor and respect, because the Muse has taught them
> Poems, and she cherishes the tribe of singers."

Who was this Homer, the bard who sang the exploits of the most famous gods and heroes of the Western tradition and who gave us our two greatest epic poems, the *Iliad* and the *Odyssey?* He might well have been several people, or he may not have existed at all; scholars have never ceased disputing the authorship of the poems attributed to him. Some say they are the work of at least two poets; some say the

Among the earliest and most renowned hero figures is Odysseus, celebrated in the latter of Homer's two immortal epics. At right, the mourning hero is depicted in a cast from a fifth-century Greek belt buckle.

Iliad is the work of the poet as a young and energetic man and the *Odyssey* that of the same poet grown older and disillusioned. Still others tell us that the epics are the result of expert patchwork by a bardic guild. In short, Homer himself is of the unknown, and in order to speak of the author of the epics mankind has therefore been obliged to create a mythic portrait of a blind poet who wandered through the Greek world singing tales of a war that took place hundreds of years before his time.

It seems likely that both the *Iliad* and the *Odyssey* were composed in the ninth century B.C. Whoever the poet was—let us call him Homer —he stitched his epics together from basic plots, from familiar elements of his people's oral tradition. Since these were chanted, several sessions would have been necessary to recite the entire *Iliad* —a poem, like the *Odyssey*, that was not written down until much later. (Indeed, it is likely that both the poet and his audience were illiterate.) This assumption is supported by the fact that both works contain a large number of stock formulae and motifs—a mnemonic device useful to the orator but hardly necessary for the reader. Thus the preparing and serving of meals is always described in one of two or three very similar and absolutely set ways. The same is true of descriptions of the rising of the sun, the taking of a bath, and the sacking of a city. In addition there are standard epithets used to describe particular characters, and each of these has a different metrical value. Clearly, as the poet chanted he chose the epithet that had the right value for the meter of the given line. And as he described a meal or a sacking in familiar, traditional terms he could be thinking ahead to the next event in his endlessly entertaining improvised narrative.

Far more than entertainment was involved here, of course. The formulae and set motifs are convenient for the poet, but they also point back to the mytho-religious origins of poetry. That there is a connection between mythic ritual and the life of the hero is evident; that the epic hero is very much a part of that ritual is particularly evident. When we consider the *Odyssey*, for example, it becomes clear that Homer was a mythmaker not only in the sense that he told or re-told stories about the gods and heroes but that, consciously or unconsciously, he used words and stories to re-create a mythic pattern in which the "Word was made flesh." As a matter of fact, the *Odyssey* itself was based on an ancient hero ritual. Appropriately, the poem begins with a discussion among the gods, one in which Athena, the goddess of wisdom and guardian spirit of Homer's wily hero, is pitted against the sea-god Poseidon, the *daimon* who launches Odysseus on the long voyage that is forever associated with his name.

In a sense, the beginning of the *Odyssey* is not only a kind of invocation but a ritual birth. The rites of childhood initiation are enacted in books one through four by Telemachus, Odysseus' son. In this section Telemachus, goaded by Athena, sets out in search of his father—and by undertaking this search for his father he symbolically searches out the hero within himself. In books five through eight the theme of the withdrawal is acted out by Odysseus himself. Telemachus may not have found his father, but the narrative has. Odysseus is first revealed to us as he sits on the island of the enchantress Calypso, longing for home. At the urging of the gods, Calypso ultimately releases Odysseus, but he lands, shipwrecked and unknown, his heroism hidden in his heart, on the island of Phaeacia. In terms of the mythic arrangement of the epic as a whole it is important that this period in the hero's life, a period in which he is unknown and humble, occur early in the poem—in spite of the fact that it belongs chronologically near the end of Odysseus' adventures. This placement suggests that Homer was working not chronologically but mythologically; the history of the universal hero had taken precedence over that of the local hero.

Spurred on by the innocent princess Nausicaa, the hospitality of the Phaeacians, and the songs of the minstrel Demodocos, Odysseus finally emerges from his stage of withdrawal and reveals his true identity. In this revelation some part of the particular hero seems to sense his role as eternal man, the representative of the human psyche. If nothing else this epic asks the question, "Who are you?" And the hero, throwing off his mask for the first time at the end of the ninth book, answers the king of Phaeacia, "I am Odysseus, son of Laertes, who for my wiles/ Am of note among all men, and my fame reaches heaven." Odysseus goes on to explain to his listeners that even the promise of immortality has not been sufficient to lure him away from his primary vision, a vision common to all who find satisfaction in their own roots:

> So nothing grows sweeter than a man's own fatherland
> And his parents, even if he dwell in a fertile home
> Far off in a foreign land apart from his parents.

Books nine through twelve of the *Odyssey* are concerned with the hero on his quest, the hero who, in the glory of his human self, defies even the gods themselves. These books relate the ritual of the adult hero, who revels in the agon of life and seeks an identifying destiny, symbolized here by hearth and home. On his quest Odysseus experi-

Two characteristics of Athena are represented in the statuette above: she wears the helmet appropriate to her status as warrior-goddess of the ancient Greeks and holds aloft the owl that symbolizes her wisdom. At right, below, the return of Odysseus to Ithaca appears on a fragmentary fifth-century relief from the island of Melos.

ences every tribulation the gods can devise. He literally travels to the ends of existence, examining the limits of the known world, the depths of the collective unconscious. He is tempted by the archetype of the femme fatale in the form of Circe and the Sirens; he must overcome the untempered animal cravings of Cyclops and the unthinking destructiveness of Scylla and Charybdis. In the Land of the Lotus Eaters, he must struggle against the natural tendency to find ease in a lack of consciousness. And, finally, he must make the ritual descent to the land of the dead, and there confront his personal destiny.

The second half of the *Odyssey* concerns the hero's return to life. Odysseus returns to Ithaca physically and spiritually renewed by his guardian, Athena; and he brings with him his son Telemachus, who is in every sense a hero himself by now, prepared to undergo the test of adult life when his father goes off, as he must, to unexplored lands. The poem ends with the inevitable heroic apotheosis, with Athena descending to raise Odysseus above the level of mortal struggle. The heroic ritual is now complete.

A significant indication of the deeply mythic nature of the ancient epics is found in their unusual style. The *Iliad* and the *Odyssey*, for example, have come down to us in a verse form that is equivalent to dactylic hexameter. This form does not suit the natural rhythm of the Greek language any better than it does that of the English language. It was, however, the language of such prophetic sanctuaries as Delphi, and it was the language of the mystery cults. It was also used at religious festivals to narrate the legends of the gods and goddesses. In short, it was the language of myth, and therefore the altogether logical choice of the epic poet in his role as mythmaker. It is a language that, when combined with epic formulae and motifs, transcended the world of the vernacular. One modern poet-critic, Robert Graves, has

gone so far as to suggest in his now classic work, *The White Goddess*, that all true poetry is based on a mythic language that is made up of a few formulae.

Whether or not Graves is correct in his theory, he touches upon something that is true about all great poetry. Homer and the other ancient bards have many spiritual descendants, not all of whom have chosen to write about gods and heroes. The emergence of basic myth has not always been dependent on culture heroes, religion, epic poems, or what we usually think of as "myths." Consider the following story in this light.

Once upon a time there reigned a king who had three sons. When the king fell desperately ill the three boys wept at their father's plight. While grieving they encountered an old man who told them, "You can save your father's life if you can find him the water of life, but the water of life is difficult to find."

The eldest son asks his father's permission to go in search of the water, but the king begs him not to go. Ultimately the king relents, however, and the prince departs, thinking as he goes, "If I find this water my father will reward me with his kingdom." The ritualistic symbolism here is clear: there are three sons, and the first is evil.

Soon the prince meets a dwarf, who asks him where he is going. "None of your business," the prince retorts, and the little man, angry at this affront, casts a spell over the prince, causing him to be trapped, still on horseback, in a narrow mountain pass. There the prince remains imprisoned.

When the eldest prince fails to return the second son asks his father's permission to go in search of the water of life. "If I find it, and if my brother is dead," he thinks, "the kingdom will be mine." The second son, too, is evil; he thinks only of personal gain.

As the second prince rides along he, too, encounters the dwarf, who asks him where he is headed. Receiving a rude answer, the dwarf treats this prince as he has the first.

When, after some time, neither brother has returned, the youngest boy seeks his father's reluctant permission to join the search for the healing water. His only concern is with his father's well-being. Clearly this is the good member of the ritual trio so familiar to readers of folk literature.

And when he meets the dwarf and is asked the ritual question he answers, "I seek the water of life, with which I hope to cure my ailing father."

"You have spoken well, without the haughtiness of your brothers," the dwarf declares, "and therefore I will tell you how to find the water. It flows from a fountain in an enchanted castle. In order to enter this castle you must have with you an iron rod and two loaves of bread." These he supplies the young man with. "The castle door will open if you knock on it three times with the rod. Inside you will confront two lions. If you give them the bread they will leave you alone. Be certain to take the water before the clock strikes twelve, or you will be imprisoned in the castle forever."

The instructions that the dwarf gives the youngest prince make no rational sense but, like all rituals, must be performed on faith. The wise old man is himself a familiar figure in fairy tales: Gilgamesh, for example, is led to the plant of eternal life by Utnapishtim, the immortal hero of the Babylonian flood myth.

Thanking the dwarf, the prince sets out on his journey and eventually arrives at the castle. Using the rod and bread, he is able to open the enchanted door and tame the lions. He then walks into a great hall in which he finds several enchanted princes. He removes the rings from their fingers and he also finds a sword and some bread. In the next room he comes upon a beautiful maiden who leads the prince to the sought-after sacred fountain.

The young prince is human, however, and therefore vulnerable. He falls asleep within sight of the fountain and awakens only moments before the great door slams shut.

Still, he is glad to have found the water, and as he journeys homeward he again passes the dwarf. When the little man sees the sword and the bread, he praises the boy on his success and informs him that with the sword he can defeat whole armies and that with the bread he can nourish himself endlessly.

The prince, being merciful and loving, begs for the release of his evil brothers, and the dwarf acquiesces. Reunited at last, the three brothers ride off; shortly thereafter, the young prince uses his newly found sword and bread to save three kingdoms from disaster.

The brothers then set sail for home, and during the voyage the evil older brothers plot against the good one. As the young prince sleeps he is robbed of the water of life, just as Gilgamesh is robbed during sleep of the plant of eternal life. The evil brothers substitute salt water for the sacred water, and as soon as the three arrive home the youngest son gives his father the sea water to drink. The king, understandably, becomes even sicker. Then the older brothers accuse their sibling of trying to murder the old man—and *they* produce the stolen water of life.

The king, believing that his youngest child has attempted to kill him, agrees to have the youth secretly murdered. We are reminded here of Shakespeare's *King Lear*, in which the same mythic situation is acted out when Lear exiles the faithful daughter Cordelia, who has been outsmarted by her ambitious and unscrupulous sisters. In both the fairy tale and the play the situation in question illustrates the fact that evil, which is nearly always active, has an advantage over good, which is often passive.

Fortunately for the king and his young son, the huntsman assigned to execute the boy cannot bring himself to carry out his orders. Like the executioner in another fairy tale, "Snow White," he releases his victim unharmed. The prince now wanders deep into the wood. Mythically speaking, he has entered a period of the ritual withdrawal. He has performed his heroic deeds, and now he must undergo the suffering that will make it possible for him to become the hero who is universal rather than local.

Soon after these events occur three cartloads of treasure arrive, tribute from the three kings the good prince had helped with his magic sword and bread. This display of gratitude leads the old king to suspect that his son may have been innocent. "How I wish he were not dead!" he exclaims. "But he lives! He lives!" cries the huntsman, who now explains to the king what he has done. The king, much relieved, sends word that his son may return to him.

Meanwhile, the princess at the enchanted castle has prepared a path of gold leading to her door, and she informs her servants that they must admit only the knight who rides to the castle on this path. The two evil brothers, remembering what their younger brother had told them, attempt to gain admittance to the castle. Both avoid riding on the gold, however, indicating that they value it over anything else. When the younger prince arrives he rides boldly up the gold path and is received into the castle. Thinking only of his beloved, he had not even noticed the path. Having emerged from a year of symbolic penance in the forest the prince is ready to take the hand of the sacred maiden.

In telling the tale of the water of life the Grimm brothers participated in the mythmaking process that is behind all great literature—indeed, behind all great art, whether ancient or modern. As the American poet Wallace Stevens wrote:

> There was a muddy center before we breathed
> There was a myth before the myth began. . . .
> From this the poem springs. . . .

And James Joyce has his hero, Stephen Dedalus, say at the end of *A Portrait of the Artist as a Young Man*, "I go to encounter for the millionth time the reality of experience and to forge in the smithy of my soul the uncreated conscience of my race." The artist, whether painter, writer, or sculptor, is nothing if not a mythmaker. When Leonardo painted *The Last Supper* and Michelangelo the ceiling of the Sistine Chapel they used Judeo-Christian symbols to give flesh to the Word, which belongs, like the hero, to everyone and no one. Assuming the ability to use the paraphernalia of a given art form, the artist, like the shaman, is successful insofar as he brings the Word to the light of consciousness—insofar as he is universal and mythic. As for his talent—the "way with words" or the "way with paint"—no one has explained that mystery better than the ancients, who attributed it to the Word itself.

The Two Americas

A lthough striking in their diversity, the myriad mythologies of the two Americas are thought by most experts to have had a common base in tribal totemism. In the north, where the climate was hostile and hunting the chief means of subsistence, this pattern was to persist well into modern times. In the south, however, clement weather and a more settled way of life were to encourage the development of far more complex and sophisticated religious rites. Among the agrarian societies of Central and South America, guardians of the harvest gradually supplanted totems of the hunt, and by the time of the Conquest these great southern civilizations had evolved elaborate cosmologies headed by an omnipotent sun-god. In central Mexico this solar deity was called Tonatiuh; in the Mayan temple-cities of the Yucatán, Hunab Ku; in the Inca strongholds of the Andes, Inti. By any name he was recognized as the greatest of natural forces and worshiped accordingly. (The Incas, for instance, believed that gold was sweat from the sun-god's brow and consecrated tons of it to his exclusive use.) Small wonder, then, that images of the sun are ubiquitous in the region: at Tiahuanaco, high on the Bolivian plateau, where a weeping sun-god carved from a mammoth block of lava surveys Titicaca, the world's highest lake; at Teotihuacán, the first metropolis in the Americas, which is dominated by a temple to Tonatiuh (seen above in a detail from a sixteenth-century Aztec manuscript); at the enigmatic Inca citadel of Machu Picchu, with its sundial called "the Hitching Place of the Sun."

By the time Hernán Cortés and his followers reached Veracruz in 1519, religious practices in Mexico had become greatly debased. At his capital of Tenochtitlán the Aztec ruler Montezuma presided over grim orgies of human sacrifice. These ritual blood-lettings necessitated nearly unending military campaigns, for Aztec victories provided the prisoners of war who became the sacrificial victims. In a sense the Aztecs captured their pantheon in the same way, adopting the local gods of the tribes they vanquished. These included the fire-god Huehueteotl (opposite), one of the most ancient deities in the Americas. Bowed beneath a brazier containing the flame of life, Huehueteotl presided over the end of each Aztec calendar cycle, a time when all fires were extinguished and a new one lit upon a prisoner's chest to urge time forward. The eight-foot-high statue at right is of Coatlicue, mother of the gods and creator of man. Thought of as a cosmic phenomenon as well as a female deity, the patroness of life and death is often depicted as a grotesque, bicephalic figure clad in a skirt of entwined snakes and a necklace of human hands and hearts. (Equally menacing is the ceremonial axehead at lower right, thought to represent a jaguar.) Among the Aztecs' adopted maize-gods was Cinteotl (below). A headdress of ripened ears encircles his brow.

Among Coatlicue's many offspring were the gods of the elements. Tlaloc, the rain-god, was originally conceived of in the most beneficent terms—as guardian of the floral bower that was life after death. In time, however, Tlaloc's sunlit, song-filled court was to acquire a sinister aspect, and his obsequies were to become the most horrific of all, as suckling infants and small children were sacrificed to a ravening rain-god (above, left) on the theory that their tears would encourage spring showers. The character of Quetzalcoatl, "the Plumed Serpent" (opposite), underwent an equally radical but far less repellent transformation over the centuries. Once a mere wind-god, Quetzalcoatl was subsequently recognized as the creator of life, patron of the arts, inventor of metallurgy, and principal deity of the Toltec pantheon. One of the principal temples of the sprawling city of Teotihuacán, built centuries before the Aztecs entered the Valley of Mexico, is dedicated to both of these sons of Coatlicue, and its stepped flanks display the serried emblems of both gods. The stele above, which once adorned that temple, depicts the rites of Quetzalcoatl, who was said to eschew human sacrifice.

Because no other religion has made human sacrifice its central ritual, none can rival that of the Aztecs in the grimness of its imagery or the grisliness of its artifacts. It is hardly necessary, for instance, to identify the statue at near right as a representation of Mictlantecuhtli, god of death; his macabre grin and skeletal limbs proclaim his role in thanatocentric pre-Conquest Mexico. Other major civilizations, notably the Egyptian, developed very elaborate funerary rites, and all evolved some concept of an afterlife; but only the Aztecs placed primacy upon the ritual slaughter of fellow beings. Armed with razor-sharp obsidian knives, the high priests of the Aztec nation would gather around the stone altars that capped their great pyramid-temples. There they would cut the still-beating hearts from a steady procession of victims (manuscript detail, far right) until the altars' runnels were clogged with gore. (The altar seen below, at center, was unearthed in the ruins of Tenochtitlán, the Aztec capital. Its function was symbolic as well as practical, as indicated by the fifty-two sheaves of cane on its base—one for every year of the Aztec "century." The corpse of Time is buried atop the altar itself under a cairn of skulls.) The hearts of those sacrificed to Tonatiuh and his insatiable myrmidons were tossed into enormous stone receptacles such as the jaguar-shaped container at lower left; the bodies were fed to carrion. As the mask at lower right suggests, Aztec cosmology was curiously bifurcated—focused simultaneously upon crops and conquest, regeneration and extirpation, ongoing life and unending destruction of life.

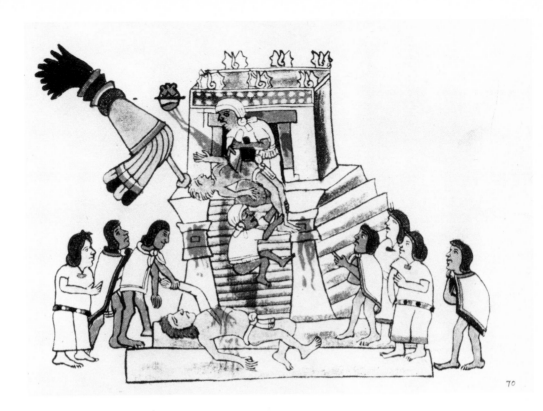

70

135

One of the most intriguing aspects of North America's native cultures is their relative youth in terms of the whole of human history. The first large-scale migrations to the Americas occurred perhaps as late as 10,000 years ago—35,000 years after man settled permanently in Western Europe—and as a result American Indian mythologies contain ritual elements long lost in more highly civilized regions of the globe. For instance, the concept of a vaguely defined Great Spirit, a nameless but prepotent celestial power, is common to all primitive societies. In Europe and the Middle East that concept was supplanted by other, more sophisticated cosmologies thousands of years ago; in North America it survived—in the oral tradition of the Algonquin and Delaware tribes, among others—well into the eighteenth century. The worship of tribal totems, likewise universal in primitive societies, also survived—on a massive scale among the Indians of the Pacific Northwest and in scaled-down versions (far left, below) elsewhere. Occasionally these totemic figures were light-hearted in design—witness the Kwakiutl Indian beaver chewing his own tail at near left—but more often their purpose was altogether serious. The carved wooden rattle at far left, center, shaped like a nesting raven and supporting a spirit figure on its back, was used by Tlingit medicine men to ward off evil spirits. The gaping mask at far left, above, served essentially the same purpose among the tribes of British Columbia. One of the most common of these totems was the Thunderbird, an eagle-headed creature that could produce thunderclaps by beating its wings and lightning by flashing its eyes. A benevolent spirit despite its fearsome appearance, the Thunderbird was revered from the forests of the Northeast to the sere mesas of the Southwest as a source of life-engendering rain, and its image was reproduced in clay and wood, colored sand and beaten silver. It was painted on bark (above), stenciled on hide, and tatooed on skin.

The Indian tribes of the Great Plains were of necessity nomadic, their migrations tied to those of the herds of bison whose flesh fed them and whose hides provided their clothing and shelter. Having no permanent homes and no fixed places of worship, these tribes carried so-called medicine bundles containing sacred charms and fetishes with them wherever they went. These hallowed packets represented the distillation of the group's unique mythic tradition, an oral history that could be reconstructed at will by the tribe's elders as they gazed at the contents of the medicine bundles. (At left, a buffalo skin upon which scenes of hunting, dancing, and warfare have been painted in a pattern intelligible only to those familiar with the history of the Dakota Sioux.) Because their survival depended upon the beneficence of nature and bounty of the hunt, the Plains Indians took special pains to propitiate the gods of natural phenomena and the spirits thought to reside in all living things. This appeal to the spirit world frequently took the form of ritual dancing, with the male members of the tribe donning fanciful costumes designed to bring rain, frighten away the Wolf Spirit, entice the salmon to shore, or lure the buffalo to his death. The masks worn on these occasions are almost infinite in their design, construction, and effect. Some, such as the pig mask at far left, below, are strictly representational; others, such as the Seneca "Crooked Mouth Mask" at near left, below, are entirely whimsical. And whereas some are exceedingly primitive—the head and antlers (below) is one of the very oldest of man's symbols—others, such as the old woman's face at lower right, are strikingly contemporary in their overall design.

6

Mythology Today

WE HAVE CONSIDERED MYTHOLOGY in the contexts of history, psychology, religion, and the creative act. We shall now consider it specifically in the context of life in the late twentieth century. To do so we must first isolate in our culture the remnants of mythological forms and themes that dominated older cultures, for only then can we move on to the mythological products of our age. What, we will ask, is the twentieth-century equivalent, in terms of the power to inform a whole civilization, of thirteenth-century Christianity in Europe or Neolithic fertility cults in the Near East? What is the "faith" that compels us to build rockets rather than cathedrals or temples? What form has the Word taken for us as a nation, as a civilization? Finally, we will look about us for the mythic trends of the future.

The most obvious place to look for the mythic in the world today is in so-called primitive societies that have been relatively untouched by modern technology. This is where anthropologists do look, finding among the South Sea Islanders, Australian aborigines, and natives of the Philippine jungle myths that incorporate many of the motifs we have discussed in this book. But modern psychology and our own experience ought to have taught us that to study the primitive human being we need not travel to Australia or the South Sea Islands. Primitive man is as accessible as our early memories and the children who live all around us. Childhood, after all, is the primary stage of an individual's development and is analogous to the primitive stage of consciousness in the history of man's development.

Children and other primitives have little or no trouble turning a bit of make-believe into reality. They are naturally mythic because to them life is still magical, unencumbered by scientific explanation; their faith in the unknown has not yet been interfered with. Water runs downhill not because of gravity but because it is bewitched; Santa Claus comes down the chimney because Santa Claus can do that sort of thing. And when a young child tells his mother that she was in his dream it makes no sense to his mythical consciousness to tell him that she was only there in his imagination.

It takes only a few moments of watching a child to know that the world of imagination and fantasy is as real to him as the rational world is to adults. The child in his daydreams and in the nightmares so common to his sleeping hours regularly experiences monsters, giants, and

The apotheosis of George Washington — sentimentally depicted on glass in a nineteenth-century burst of American patriotism—is a notable example of modern mythologizing at work.

141

various mythical adventures. Furthermore, children are mythical in their search for origins and for security in a dangerous world. When he asks his parents to "tell me about when you were little," the child is demanding a mythic history. The father and mother who emerge from the resulting stories of the past are immortals of a marvelous, distant, golden age. The heroic quality of parents is further indicated in such remarks as "my father can beat up your father" and "my mother is more beautiful than your mother." If children fail to break out of this stage we say of them, using traditional mythic stories, that they suffer from Oedipus or Electra complexes. Finally, children, like all primitive, mythically conscious people, are highly ritualistic. Their psychic security depends on things being done a certain way. There can be no substitute for certain blankets, night-lights, spoons, ways of dressing, ways of saying good-night, and so on.

At a certain age children are told they must "grow up." The special pacifier must be discarded; the night-light must be turned off; Santa Claus must be seen for what he really is. But even this scrubbing away of magic does not destroy the mythic instincts. As primitive people, whether whole tribes or individual children, become more developed, more conscious, they simply transfer these instincts. One place to which they transfer them is organized religion. When a religious person enters a church or temple, at least in theory, he leaves the rational world of getting and spending and behaves in a manner that the uninitiated might well consider ridiculous.

Religious rituals are performed not in the name of reason but in the name of something called faith. Faith is mythic; it becomes real only through a primitive, childlike suspension of disbelief. "Except ye be converted and become as little children, ye shall not enter into the kingdom of heaven." It is not insignificant that within the church even people very much of the world play ritual games in which certain things become what they are not and statues, like dolls, are spoken to. Furthermore, churchgoers confess to having been bad and are forgiven and advised on how to be good by men they sometimes call "father." In effect, the worshiper acknowledges by his presence and

Mythic creatures guard the holy places of medieval Europe and ancient China: bizarre gargoyles atop Notre-Dame de Paris (left) and a splendidly imaginative lion at the gateway to Peking's Forbidden City (right).

behavior in the place of worship that he needs mythic experience, a need that is not tolerated and often is not accepted in the real world —at least not beyond childhood.

In orthodox religions, the place of worship itself is appropriately mythic. The traditional Gothic cathedral of Catholicism is a good example. Shaped like a Latin cross, the church proper stands for the body of Christ. On the outside of the church are pagan gargoyles, placed there to remind the worshiper that he, like the hero, is entering upon a passage to the other world—a world of death out of which can come new life. So Christ brings Adam through the jaws of a dragon into paradise; so Moses passes through the parted Red Sea. Ferocious temple guardians are common to many religious traditions, and they nearly always stand at the entrances to the underworlds of the various mythic traditions.

Having passed through the doors—having been "born" into Christ —the Catholic worshiper finds himself at the base of the cross that is the building. Here, in the narthex, is a small container of holy water. By dipping his fingers into it and making the sign of the cross upon himself, he symbolically repeats the sacrament of baptism, through which, as a child, he was initiated into the sacred fellowship. In a universal sense he purifies himself for the heroic journey, as Christ did when he had himself baptized by John the Baptist. Entering the nave—the lofty, central section of the church—the worshiper discovers the baptismal font, a further reminder of his childhood initiation. It is here in the center of the symbolic body of Christ that the ritual acts of heroic withdrawal and quest will be performed. Through prayer, self-examination, assistance from those wiser than himself, and a sharing in the scriptures of the quest for eternal life, the initiate is prepared to participate in the life-giving mystery that celebrates Christ's sacrifice. When he eats the bread and drinks the wine, the Christian experiences Christ's death—and in doing so he is reborn. The sacrificial act itself takes place in the sanctuary, the "head" of the symbolic church-body. The altar on which the bread and wine become the body and blood of Christ is symbolic of both the table of the Last Supper—at which Jesus instituted the sacrament of Holy Communion—and of the tomb out of which his body rose from the dead. Standing on a raised platform, it also signifies the throne of God to which Christ ascended.

It should be evident that the Catholic liturgy and the church building itself embody a mythic purpose that transcends any single religion. Christ is a version of the universal hero and his church is a symbol of the cosmic world view implicit in the hero myth. Moving from entrance to altar, the worshiper moves with all true heroes from the earthbound life of this world to the liberation of union with ultimate reality. He moves from the monsters that threaten the child, to the water in which the hero is abandoned to us all, to the tree on which he is sacrificed as a scapegoat. Through such symbols the Christian, the Buddhist, the Jew—indeed, any worshiper—attempts to open himself at least temporarily to an experience of the Word.

But mythology is not confined to childhood or churchgoing. It is very much in evidence in the secular world of adults. A relatively obvious example is television advertising, for advertisers are successful only insofar as they are able to tap the universal language of mythology. When a particular actor appears on the screen in the guise of the friendly family doctor we are confronted by a modern mythic being. Polls show that as a society we place more faith in our doctors than we do in our priests or our teachers. The friendly family doctor is the Merlin of our technological age, and as long as we believe in him his medicine can be remarkably effective regardless of its content. The wise old man in the fairy tale tells the young prince that he must knock three times with an iron rod for the door to open—an instruction, we have already noted, that is ritualistic or magical rather than rational. Investigations show that one third of people with minor illnesses experience immediate relief by taking the medicine prescribed for them by their physicians, suggesting that their complaints are as much functional as actual—and highly susceptible to magical cures.

Problems arise, in fact, when such faith—and such myths—are undermined. The individual who no longer has faith in medicine is likely to find that medicine has lost its curative powers. In the same way political scandal shows us how painful it can be when a society's political myths are destroyed. Kings and presidents, like religious leaders, embody social myths, and if it becomes inescapably evident that they are corrupt—that they do not practice what they preach—the very fabrics of the societies to which they are answerable are profoundly affected.

Another example of the function of mythology in our culture can be found in nationalism—a force that developed out of nineteenth-century European Romanticism and that, like any other mythic force, has claimed the allegiance and the lives of millions. The myth of nationalism, of course, takes many external forms. Such terms as the "American way," the "American dream," and "American know-how," for example, are products of one of these forms, the American myth. The hero of this myth is Davey Crockett or Daniel Boone, conquerors of the frontier—which is itself described by historians and storytellers

The great hero of the Bolshevik Revolution, Lenin (above) has been virtually deified by Russia's Soviet government; along with Karl Marx and Friedrich Engels, he forms what amounts to a holy trinity of communist ideology. In the United States modern mythmaking continues with the idealization of political leaders—most notably, Abraham Lincoln. The anonymous artist of the work opposite had a simple task: he merely substituted Lincoln's face for that of Washington in the "apotheosis" painting reproduced on page 140.

as pervasively mythic. He is the Horatio Alger hero rising from rags to riches, and he is the rustic figure of the tall tale who uses his ingenuity to outsmart the Old World sophisticates. Perhaps most important of all, he is the American president, who is expected to embody whatever it is that informs and defines American culture. In an earlier chapter we spoke of the myths associated with George Washington, the "father of our country." Our own century has produced a president whose fate it was to become mythic in an all too tragic manner. John Kennedy, the first president born in this century, was expected to change the world with his new vision. His administration was associated with King Arthur's Camelot, and his death was a protracted, anguished, heroic pageant. Furthermore, out of the young president's death came a sense of national unity—a rebirth of the American myth— as people of all classes and political parties watch the fairy-tale cortege move through Washington.

Probably the most popular embodiment of the American myth is "The Great Emancipator," Abe Lincoln. It is significant that he is more often "Abe" than Abraham. Is the aristocratic Thomas Jefferson ever "Tom"? Abe Lincoln, like "Ben" Franklin and the Horatio Alger hero, symbolizes a particular aspect of the American dream, its classlessness. Out of the self-made-man myth that Lincoln personified came the modern American sociological myth of "upward mobility" in

which "success," based on the "Protestant work ethic," is the goal of a national quest. The place of adventure—the hunting ground—for the new American hero has been the city; his Eden, suburbia. Perhaps the ultimate symbol of upward mobility is the spaceship, departing explosively and expensively from a chaotic world. Back in suburbia, however, the primary mythic symbol is the home, which is a "man's castle" presided over by a woman who has been carried ritualistically over its threshold.

Naturally the American myth does not work for everyone. All Moms are not Earth Mothers, and relatively few people achieve the success goal. But it is only when the goal ceases to exist as a possibility, when it no longer informs one's life, that the myth dies as a psychological reality and becomes simply a myth in the sense that an old wives' tale is a myth. The poorest house is a castle as long as its inhabitants retain faith in the myth, but as soon as the faith is lost the castle becomes an imprisoning, unloved ghetto. And when faith in one myth dissipates, people instinctively search for a new myth to take its place. This explains the nationalist movements that surfaced in Eastern Europe, Africa, and Southeast Asia following World War II. And it explains the current search of America's minority groups for a sense of their own identity.

Basic to the American myth and to all other national myths is the abstract concept of the nation as an organic and sometimes almost conscious entity. Thus we speak of the "birth" of a nation, of the "father" of a nation, of the "motherland" and the "fatherland." And we further personify nations with symbols such as Uncle Sam or John Bull. To the nationalist the nation is something with an almost godlike power to receive and appreciate adulation and sacrifice. The national flag, for example, contains something that transcends its material nature: it represents roots and identity.

As we have seen, the Word wears many masks, is made flesh in

National mythmaking is exemplified in the assigning of personalities to countries—such as England's John Bull and the United States' Uncle Sam (left). Alternatively, nation states are represented by zoomorphic figures; in the 1900 Puck cartoon opposite, above, the Russian bear, American eagle, and British lion, among others, fight over the prostrate body of the Chinese dragon—a comment on late-nineteenth-century Western dismemberment of that hapless nation. Ranked as king of the birds, the eagle has commonly been used as a heraldic device; right, the double-headed eagle adopted by Prussia's royal house, an appropriately bellicose symbol for that expansionist state.

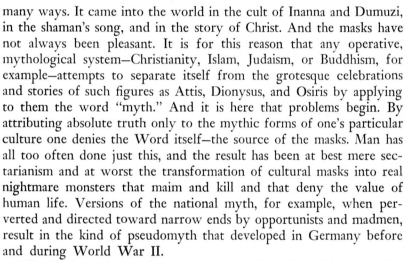

many ways. It came into the world in the cult of Inanna and Dumuzi, in the shaman's song, and in the story of Christ. And the masks have not always been pleasant. It is for this reason that any operative, mythological system—Christianity, Islam, Judaism, or Buddhism, for example—attempts to separate itself from the grotesque celebrations and stories of such figures as Attis, Dionysus, and Osiris by applying to them the word "myth." And it is here that problems begin. By attributing absolute truth only to the mythic forms of one's particular culture one denies the Word itself—the source of the masks. Man has all too often done just this, and the result has been at best mere sectarianism and at worst the transformation of cultural masks into real nightmare monsters that maim and kill and that deny the value of human life. Versions of the national myth, for example, when perverted and directed toward narrow ends by opportunists and madmen, result in the kind of pseudomyth that developed in Germany before and during World War II.

The Nazi myth contains many aspects of traditional mythologies. Much of it sprang from German legends revived by the composer Richard Wagner in his operas. Two themes were especially important in Wagner's stories and in the Nazi myth: the cult of the Nordic race and the cult of the sacred soil. Wagner's blond and blue-eyed Siegfried would emerge in the Nazi world view as the archetype of the heroic supermen who were to dominate a world purged of the Jew. The leader of the new heroes had the godlike, superhero qualities of omnipotence and infallibility. To give themselves roots the Nazis stressed a mythic line of Prussian heroes that moved from Siegfried to Frederick the Great to Bismarck to Hindenburg to Hitler.

Out of the cult of the soil grew a horrendous parody of the romantic ideal of the living nation-state. To the Nazis, of course, the fatherland was not a perversion of national pride but the future seat of an Aryan paradise. Like another twentieth-century ideology, communism, with its promise of a classless millennium, and like much of modern nationalism, the Nazi credo contained the Messianic and historical perspectives so basic to the Judeo-Christian tradition. Basic to this tradition is the concept of a time to come, a time in the historical future, when a people chosen of God and led by a Messiah will be welcomed into paradise.

There are many who would say that the Judeo-Christian tradition no longer provides a sustaining life-force in the Western world—that in fact it has been in the process of being displaced as the dominant mythic mask since the Age of Reason in the late seventeenth century. If this is so, what has taken its place? A significant aspect of the Western world view since the seventeenth century has been the belief in the possibility that there is no conscious, controlling force in the universe. The possibility exists, therefore, that in the modern world the Word need not take the form of gods, heroes, and adventures. Indeed, Theodore Roszak has suggested that the myth of our culture has instead taken the form of a mode of thinking that he calls "objective consciousness." From the days of our childhood we are told that we can do anything as long as we "put our minds to it." And since the Age of Reason we have increasingly accepted on faith the idea that the way of objectivity leads to all that is known or can eventually be known.

If the world view of the Inanna cult was the measuring rod of Sumer, and the world view of Christianity was the measuring rod of the West in the Middle Ages, the staff against which modern experience is measured is the world view of the scientist. In this even our religious leaders conspire by rationalizing or denying outright miracles. Such stories as Christ's virgin birth and his resurrection become symbolic rather than actual realities because they cannot be explained by reason, which is to say because they cannot be assimilated into the myth of objective consciousness. This myth, to which twentieth-century man has surrendered with the unquestioning faith once reserved for religion, is embodied not by the priests and rabbis to whom we listen for an hour or so once a week, but by the doctors, scientists, and military men who do their jobs with as little emotional involvement as possible.

In recent years the myth of objective consciousness—the scientific myth—has itself come under attack. Its critics warn us that our miraculous cures have opened the way to worse disease, that our technocratic approach to problems has polluted our environment and depleted our resources. The point, say these critics, is that objectivity in itself is not a path to truth. Like the national and religious myths it is but a mask for the Word—a mask our culture put on when it was needed and now has worn out. To believe we can solve our energy problems by finding new sources of fossil fuel or by harnessing atomic power is simply to indulge in a superstition of a dying myth. And thus we have a kind of religious war between an older generation that places its faith in technological advances and their more "idealistic" children.

Naturally the critics of objective consciousness comprise a minority even among young people. Myths die slowly. Most people go on in the old way, according to the old values, and often they twist and pervert

Twentieth-century mythmaking achieved an obscene crescendo with the Nazi glorification of the so-called Aryan race and the absurd and ultimately destructive perversion of German national pride that was the basis for Hitler's Third Reich. In the Nazi recruiting poster above, an idealized, brawny, blue-eyed blond youth represents a Hitler student group.

the old mythologies to greater and greater absurdities. It is, then, to the counter culture that we must turn in order to determine the nature of the mythology of the future.

To begin with, there seems to be a consensus among critics of modern culture as to the need for what they call myth consciousness. The myth of objective consciousness, they feel, is in reality antimythic in the sense that by its avoidance of anything transcendental it suppresses a very real human need for contact with the universal rhythms contained in older mythologies. In our obeisance to objectivity, say the new mythmakers, we have buried the universal cosmic Word in the name of merely human words. We have been guilty, like the ancient tragic heroes, of the sin of hubris, or overweening pride. Our allegiance to rationalism has made it impossible for us to respond to cosmic symbols and realities and has left us prey to the psychic "underworld."

The new thinkers have therefore attempted to break through the barriers of objective consciousness—a difficult task, for the myth's hold on us is tight indeed—in order to re-achieve contact with the long-neglected vitality all around us. In order to do so, the mythmakers have sought to put old myths into perspective and make them useful as a framework for a new mythology. Christ used Judaism and the Buddha Hinduism in this fashion.

It is hardly surprising, then, that emerging myth appears to involve a marriage between science and religion. This marriage leads not to a narrow adherence to a particular sect or to the scientific view, but rather to something the new mythmakers call "consciousness expansion." The new believer may be a Christian, a Jew, a Buddhist, or a Taoist, but he recognizes that these sects are but individual expressions of the universal Word. He may also be a scientist, but he understands that the true science is not that of the Manhattan Project but that of the Pythagorean "music of the spheres"—of a scientific order that is ultimately beyond reason.

A leading prophet of the new mythology was Swiss psychiatrist Carl Jung, a man of science who realized the importance of the transcendent to the human psyche and who tried to lead modern man back to myth consciousness. In 1914 Jung experienced a long period of disorientation. At the time, Western Europe was edging toward World War I, and the seams of Western culture were beginning to come apart. Jung, like any prophet or shaman of the past, was simply mirroring the malaise of his time—but being a scientist, he decided on an experiment. He would find some way of consciously "submitting" himself to the impulses of the unconscious and would thus be led to a way of overcoming his disorientation—or so he hoped.

A childhood memory of building blocks and mud castles came to Jung's mind, and he experienced the emotional fascination that the acts of creation associated with these objects had once given him. He realized that the uninhibited boy who still existed within his psyche possessed a creative mythic life that could help him with his current problem. To the scientist it seemed obvious that the best way to re-establish contact with that primitive, mythic creativity was to re-create as closely as possible the circumstances that had originally stimulated it.

To this end Jung overcame the rational adult resistance to childhood games and begin to work daily on a miniature mud, sand, and stone village along the shore of a nearby lake. Gradually, through absorption in his task, he was able to understand the fantasies of his primitive nature. He realized that such irrational game-playing was analogous to religious ritual, and that by playing in this way he was "on the way to discerning my own myth." The childhood fantasy games were the beginning of a long, heroic journey into the unknown of Jung's own psyche.

In speaking of it later Jung described what sounds like a shamanic flight or descent:

In order to seize hold of the fantasies, I frequently imagined a steep descent. I even made several attempts to get to the very bottom. The first time I reached, as it were, a depth of about a thousand feet; the next time I found myself at the edge of a cosmic abyss. It was like a voyage to the moon, or a descent into empty space.

And, like the shaman in the other world and the hero in the underworld or labyrinth, Jung found that he could escape from the fantasy world "only by extreme effort." Only by keeping up his clinical practice—by retaining contact with the day-to-day concerns of his worldly profession—could he manage to escape. This was indeed a dangerous experiment, but by confronting the unconscious head-on Jung was able to rediscover "the matrix of a mythopoetic imagination which has vanished from our rational age." He could make use of this imagination in his clinic, and under his guidance disoriented patients could be exposed to it, could rediscover themselves by achieving contact with their "dark sides." The world of myth, dream, and religion could be brought to the light of consciousness.

A second prophet of this new mythology was Pierre Teilhard de Chardin, who as both a Jesuit priest and a paleontologist was himself a paradigm of the marriage of science and religion. Teilhard is perhaps the major theoretician of the new mythology, for he formulated the mystical-scientific myth that Jung's work pointed to. He began from the position that mankind is a phenomenon of the universe and thus is in a constant process of "becoming." Human beings are, like flowers and mountains, *of* the earth.

As Alan Watts, a later popularizer of Teilhard's ideas, wrote, "The truth of the matter is that you didn't come *into* this world at all. You came *out* of it, in just the same way that a leaf comes out of a tree or a baby from a womb." Furthermore, said Watts, "we have lacked the real humility of recognizing that we are members of the biosphere . . . in which we cannot exist at all without the cooperation of plants, insects, fish, cattle, and bacteria."

In Teilhard's evolutionary process of becoming everything is potentially more than it presently is. We evolved from single-cell animals; thus all organisms contain the potential for higher life. Man is still in the process of completion, still on his way to a higher state of consciousness. According to Teilhard, God's special gift to man—that which distinguishes him from other phenomena of nature—is his capacity to remain a single interbreeding species and thus to concentrate and speed up his evolutionary development. Birds, for example, have in a sense dissipated their evolutionary energy by breaking up into several thousand noninterbreeding species.

The eventual result of man's evolutionary concentration, in Teilhard's view, will be the emergence of a single, global community populated by humans who have achieved a sufficiently high level of consciousness to realize their total relationship to the biosphere. They will realize they are not subjects of a blind process; that the world is, as Alan Watts has described it, a "vast pattern of intelligent energy"; and that people "are not *in* it at all," they "*are* it." Living according to this new and mystical myth, it will be possible to be local in small, self-sufficient, decentralized communities and universal in recognizing that these communities reflect a self-sufficient and decentralized planet. In what one new mythmaker, William Thompson, has called the "planetary culture," the new man will have "transcended individuality in personality"; like the hero of the old myths, he will have become in fact "universal man."

As idealistic and irrational as Teilhard's view might seem, it is based on realities that are becoming increasingly clear. To begin with, as our chapter on the hero made apparent, we have always been, in the deepest sense, one world. Second, modern technology has brought the peoples of the world into closer proximity. As a result it has become increasingly difficult for any one group to think it possesses the only truth. As we learn more about the Far East, for example, we are less likely to think of Taoism or Buddhism as mere superstitions. The religious spirit of our time is clearly ecumenical; people are recognizing the universal meaning behind the sectarian symbols. And, finally, the ecological crises of recent years have demonstrated our interdependence and the absurdity of placing sectarian interests before human interests.

The time of the new mythology would seem to have arrived. We can, of course, refuse to live by it; we can meet across the disappearing horizons with weapons, and at such close quarters we are bound to destroy one another. Or, we can meet "as little children," recognizing in one another—whoever or whatever we are—the "Word made flesh." When we do the latter the world myth—the myth of the voyage to self-knowledge—will have come to life.

152

IN THE BEGINNING

Creation Myths Around the World

The imaginative and touching portrait of God as architect of the universe, opposite, graces a thirteenth-century French manuscript edition of the Bible.

The Bible's Book of Genesis needs no introduction; the initial words of the text are instantly recognizable. In the story of God's creation of the world in six days we have the most lucid of man's many creation myths. Although it is difficult to establish either age or authorship of the Old Testament with any certainty, scholars have ascribed the Book of Genesis to an anonymous Judaean who lived in the eighth century B.C.

In the beginning God created the heaven and the earth.

And the earth was without form, and void; and darkness was upon the face of the deep. And the Spirit of God moved upon the face of the waters.

And God said, Let there be light: and there was light.

And God saw the light, that it was good: and God divided the light from the darkness.

And God called the light Day, and the darkness he called Night. And the evening and the morning were the first day.

And God said, Let there be a firmament in the midst of the waters, and let it divide the waters from the waters.

And God made the firmament, and divided the waters which were under the firmament from the waters which were above the firmament: and it was so.

And God called the firmament Heaven. And the evening and the morning were the second day.

And God said, Let the waters under the heaven be gathered together unto one place, and let the dry land appear: and it was so.

And God called the dry land Earth; and the gathering together of the waters called he Seas: and God saw that it was good.

And God said, Let the earth bring forth grass, the herb yielding seed, and the fruit tree yielding fruit after his kind, whose seed is in itself, upon the earth: and it was so.

And the earth brought forth grass, and herb yielding seed after his kind, and the tree yielding fruit, whose seed was in itself, after his kind; and God saw that it was good.

And the evening and the morning were the third day.

And God said, Let there be lights in the firmament of the heaven to divide the day from the night; and let them be for signs, and for seasons, and for days, and years;

And let them be for lights in the firmament of the heaven to give light upon the earth: and it was so.

And God made two great lights: the greater light to rule the day, and the lesser light to rule night: he made the stars also.

And God set them in the firmament of the heaven to give light upon the earth.

And to rule over the day and over the night, and to divide the light from the darkness: and God saw that it was good.

And the evening and the morning were the fourth day.

And God said, Let the waters bring forth abundantly the moving creature that hath life, and fowl that may fly above the earth in the open firmament of heaven.

And God created great whales, and every living creature that moveth, which the waters brought forth abundantly, after their kind, and every winged fowl after his kind: and God saw that it was good.

And God blessed them, saying, Be fruitful, and multiply, and fill the waters in the seas, and let fowl multiply in the earth.

And the evening and the morning were the fifth day.

And God said, Let the earth bring forth the living creature after his kind, cattle, and creeping thing, and beast of the earth after his kind: and it was so.

And God made the beast of the earth after his kind, and cattle after their kind, and every thing that creepeth upon the earth after his kind: and God saw that it was good.

And God said, Let us make man in our image, after our likeness; and let them have dominion over the fish of the sea, and over the fowl of the air, and over the cattle, and over all the earth, and over every creeping thing that creepeth upon the earth.

So God created man in his own image, in the image of God created he him; male and female created he them.

And God blessed them, and God said unto them, Be fruitful, and multiply, and replenish the earth, and subdue it; and have dominion over the fish of the sea, and over the fowl of the air, and over every living thing that moveth upon the earth.

And God said, Behold, I have given you every herb bearing seed, which is upon the face of all the earth, and every tree, in the which is the fruit of a tree yielding seed; to you it shall be for meat.

And to every beast of the earth, and to every fowl of the air, and to every thing that creepeth upon the earth, wherein there is life, I have given every green herb for meat: and it was so.

And God saw every thing that he had made, and behold, it was very good. And the evening and the morning were the sixth day.

Thus the heavens and the earth were finished, and all the host of them.

And on the seventh day God ended his work which he had made; and he rested on the seventh day from all his work which he had made.

And God blessed the seventh day, and sanctified it: because that in it he had rested from all his work which God created and made.

These are the generations of the heavens and of the earth when they were created, in the day that the Lord God made the earth and the heavens.

And every plant of the field before it was in the earth, and every herb of the field before it grew: for the Lord God had not caused it to rain upon the earth, and there was not a man to till the ground.

But there went up a mist from the earth, and watered the whole face of the ground.

And the Lord God formed man of the dust of the ground, and breathed into his nostrils the breath of life; and man became a living

The Book of Genesis has been a constant and continuing source of inspiration to Western artists. The panel above is the first of a series of illuminations from a thirteenth-century French Bible that relates the Judeo-Christian creation story; others are reproduced on the following pages.

soul.

And the Lord God planted a garden eastward in Eden; and there he put the man whom he had formed.

And out of the ground made the Lord God to grow every tree that is pleasant to the sight, and good for food; the tree of life also in the midst of the garden, and the tree of knowledge of good and evil.

And a river went out of Eden to water the garden; and from thence it was parted, and became into four heads.

The name of the first is Pison: that is it which compasseth the whole land of Havilah, where there is gold;

And the gold of that land is good: there is bdellium and the onyx stone.

And the name of the second river is Gihon: the same is it that compasseth the whole land of Ethiopia.

And the name of the third river is Hiddekel: that is it which goeth toward the east of Assyria. And the fourth river is Euphrates.

And the Lord God took the man, and put him into the garden of Eden to dress it and to keep it.

And the Lord God commanded the man, saying, Of every tree of the garden thou mayest freely eat:

But of the tree of the knowledge of good and evil, thou shalt not eat of it: for in the day that thou eatest thereof thou shalt surely die.

And the Lord God said, It is not good that the man should be alone; I will make him an help meet for him.

And out of the ground the Lord God formed every beast of the field and every fowl of the air: and brought them unto Adam to see what he would call them: and whatsoever Adam called every living creature that was the name thereof.

And Adam gave names to all cattle, and to the fowl of the air, and to every beast of the field; but for Adam there was not found an help meet for him.

And the Lord God caused a deep sleep to fall upon Adam, and he slept: and he took one of his ribs, and closed up the flesh instead thereof;

And the rib, which the Lord God had taken from man, made he a woman, and brought her unto the man.

And Adam said, This is now bone of my bones, and flesh of my flesh: she shall be called Woman, because she was taken out of Man.

Therefore shall a man leave his father and his mother, and shall cleave unto his wife: and they shall be one flesh.

And they were both naked, the man and his wife, and were not ashamed.

GENESIS 1–2

The Babylonian Enûma elish *("When above") is only incidentally a creation myth. The epic's primary purpose was to offer cosmological evidence in support of Marduk's position at the head of the Babylonian pantheon.*

Thus the work opens with the birth of the gods within the commingled waters of the primeval parents, Apsû and Ti'âmat. The clamor of these offspring disturbs Apsû and, over Ti'âmat's protests, he resolves to kill them. But the clever Ea, "who fathoms everything," learns of his father's plans and slays him. Ti'âmat, enraged by the murder of her husband, vows to avenge him. She bears a brood of eleven monster-serpents to assist her in a war against the gods. The gods, terrified, beg Ea's son Marduk to be their champion. He agrees to do so, but only in return for supremacy over them. Marduk vanquishes Ti'âmat, and creates heaven and earth by cleaving her carcass in two. From the blood of Ti'âmat's former commander, Kingu, Marduk and Ea create mankind. The epic concludes with a long exaltation to the almighty Marduk. Enûma elish was composed in the second millennium B.C., *and many scholars have found analogies between it and the first two chapters of Genesis.**

When above the heaven had not (yet) been named,
(And) below the earth had not (yet) been called by a name;
(When) only Apsû primeval, their begetter, (existed),
(And) mother Ti'âmat, who gave birth to them all;
(When) their waters (still) mingled together,
(And) no dry land had been formed (and) not (even) a marsh could
    be seen;
When none of the gods had been brought into being,
(When) they had not (yet) been called by (their) name(s, and their)
    destinies had not (yet) been fixed:
Then were the gods created in the midst of them.
Lahmu and Lahâmu they brought into being; they were called by
    (their) names.
For ages they grew (and) became lofty.
Anshar and Kishwar were created, they surpassed them.
Many days passed, the years increased.
Anu was their son, the rival of his fathers;
To Anshar his first-born, Anu, became equal.
And Anu begat Nudimmud, his image.
Nudimmud, the master of his fathers was he,
Endowed with understanding, wise, mighty in strength,
Much stronger than his grandfather, Anshar;
He had no rival among the gods, his brothers.
The divine brothers banded themselves together;
They disturbed Ti'âmat and assaulted their keeper;
Indeed, they caused pain to the heart of Ti'âmat,
Moving (and) running about in the divine abode(?).

*Because of the fragmentary nature of the original text, the translator and editors have made use of the following symbols:
    ( ) enclose elements not in the original but desirable or necessary
        for a better understanding in English
    (?) meaning is uncertain
    [ ] enclose restorations in the text
    . . . . indicates text is unintelligible to translator, or that superfluous material
        has been cut
    [. . . .] indicates text is damaged and therefore unintelligible

Apsû diminished not their clamor,
Also Ti'âmat acquiesced [in it . .] . . ,
Yet their doings were annoying [to them].
Their way was not good . . . . .
Then Apsû, the begetter of the great gods,
Cried out and called Mummu, his vizier, (saying:)
"Mummu, my vizier, who rejoicest my heart,
Come to me, let us go to Ti'âmat!"
They went and sat down before Ti'âmat;
They took counsel together concerning the gods, their first-born.
Apsû opened his mouth
And said to Ti'âmat, the holy(?) one:
"Their way is annoying to me,
By day I cannot rest, by night I cannot sleep;
I will destroy (them) and put an end to their way,
That silence be established, and then let us rest!"
When Ti'âmat heard this,
She was wroth and cried out to her husband;
She cried out and raged furiously, she alone.
(For) the malice of (Apsû) disturbed her heart.
"Why should we destroy that which we have brought forth?
Their way is indeed very annoying, but let us take it good-
    humoredly!"
Mummu spoke up and counseled Apsû;
[Hostile (?)] and unfavorable was the advice of his Mummu:
"Yes, my father, destroy (their) disturbing way;
Then verily thou shalt find rest by day and sleep by night!"
When Apsû heard it, his face grew bright,
Because of the evil he planned against the gods, his sons,
Mummu embraced his neck,
Sat down on his knees (and) kissed him.
Whatever they planned in their assembly
Was communicated to the gods, their first-born.
When the gods heard (it), they were agitated;
They took to silence, they sat quietly.
The most excellent in understanding, the wise (and) skilful,
Ea, who fathoms everything, saw through their plan.
He made and established against it a (magic) drawing for all
    (eventualities);
He composed a most holy incantation of artistic beauty,
He recited it and caused it to be upon the water.
He (thus) poured out sleep upon him, (and) he lay sound asleep.
After he had caused Apsû to lie down and (Apsû) was asleep.
Mummu, the adviser, he . . . . .
He loosened his garment, tore off his crown,
He carried off his rays (and) put (them) [on] himself.
He fettered Apsû and slew him;
Mummu he bound (and) locked him up.

He established upon Apsû his dwelling-place,
And Mummu he seized for himself, holding his nose-rope.
After [Ea] had vanquished (and) subdued his enemies,
(And) had established his victory over his foes,
In his abode composedly he rested;
He named it *Apsû* and appointed (it) for shrines.
In that place he caused his chamber to be founded;
Ea (and) Damkina, his wife, dwelt (therein) in splendor.
In the chamber of fates, the abode of destinies,
The most skilful, the wisest of the gods, [was begotten (?)],
Within the *Apsû* Marduk was born,
Within the holy *Apsû* [Marduk] was born.
He who begot him was [Ea], his father;
Damkina, his mother, was she who bore him;
He sucked the breast of goddesses;
The nurse that cared for him filled (him) with awe-inspiring majesty.
Enticing was his form, flashing the glance of his eyes,
Lordly was his going-forth, a leader from of old.
When [Ea], his father that begot (him), saw him,
He rejoiced, he beamed, his heart was filled with joy.
He distinguished (?) him and conferred upon [him] a twofold god-
    head,
(So that) he was highly exalted (and) surpassed them in every way.
Beautiful beyond comprehension were his members,
Not fit for (human) understanding, hard (for the eyes) to look upon.
Four were his eyes, four were his ears.
When he moved his lips, fire blazed forth.
(His) four ears grew large,
Also (his) eyes, likewise four, (and) seeing everything.
He was exalted among the gods, surpassing was his form;
His members were gigantic, highly surpassing was he.
Mâri-ûtu, Mâri-ûtu:
Son of the sun-god, son of the sun of the gods.
He was clothed with the rays of ten gods, exceedingly strong was he;
[The awe-inspiring maj]esty of their flashing splendor was heaped
    upon him. . . .
Disturbed was Ti'âmat, and day and night she hastened about.
They planned evil in their heart;
To Ti'âmat the brothers said,
"When they slew Apsû, thy spouse,
Thou didst not march at his side, but thou didst sit quietly. . . .
Remember(?) Apsû, thy husband,
And Mummu, who were vanquished; thou alone remainest. . . .

*The gods incite Ti'âmat to avenge the deaths of Apsû and Mummu. She
creates eleven monster-serpents to aid in the forthcoming battle against the
offending gods.*

Of those among the gods, her first-born, who gathered [around her],

She exalted Kingu; in their midst she made him great.

To go before the host, to direct the forces,

To raise the weapons for the engagement, to advance to the attack,

The high-command of the battle,

She intrusted to him; she caused him to sit in the assembly (saying:)

"I have uttered the incantation for thee, I have magnified thee in the assembly of the gods.

The dominion over all the gods I have given into thy hand.

Mayest thou be exalted, thou, my chosen spouse!

May thy names become greater than (those of) all the Anunnak.

She gave him the tablet of destinies, she fastened (it) upon his breast, (saying:)

"As for thee, thy command shall not be changed, [the word of thy mouth] shall be established!"

Now when Kingu had been exalted (and) had received [supreme dominion],

To the gods, her(!) sons, [they decreed] the destinies, (saying:)

"May the opening of your mouth vanquish the fire-god!

(But) when Anu [drew nigh] and saw Ti'âmat's frame of mind,

[He could not stand before her and] he turned back.

[He went in terror to] his [father,] Anshar.

[Concerning Ti'âmat thus] he spoke to him:

"[Rem]ove from me the hands with which thou art holding (me)!"

Anshar lapesd into silence, looking upon the ground.

. . . . shaking his head at Ea.

All the Anunnaki were assembled at the place.

Their lips were closed, they sat in silence.

"There is no god who can go t[o battle and]

From the presence of Ti'âmat escape w[ith his life]."

Lord Anshar, the father of the gods, [arose in] majesty,

After he had pondered in his heart, and he s[aid to the Anunna]ki,

"He whose [strength] is mighty shall be [our] champion.

[That one is] the scourge(?) of conflict, the mighty Marduk!"

Ea called [Marduk] to his private room;

[He ad]vised (him), telling him the plan of his heart:

"O Marduk, consider my idea, hearken to thy father.

Thou art he, my son, who gladdens his heart;

Draw nigh into the presence of Anshar, (ready) for battle;

Speak (and) stand forth; when he beholds thee he will be at rest."

The lord rejoiced at the word of his father;

He drew nigh and stood before Anshar.

When Anshar saw him, his heart was filled with joy;

He kissed his lips, and his fear was removed.

"[Anshar,] be not silent, (but) open thy lips;

I will go and accomplish all that is in thy heart.

[Yea, Anshar,] be not silent, (but) open thy lips;

[I will] go and accomplish all that is in thy heart!

What man is it who has brought battle against thee?

[. . . .] Ti'âmat, who is a woman, is coming against thee with arms!
[My father(?),] creator, rejoice and be glad;
Soon thou shalt trample upon the neck of Ti'âmat.
[Yea, my father(?),] creator, rejoice and be glad;
Soon thou shalt trample upon the [neck] of Ti'âmat!"
"My son, who knowest all wisdom,
Quiet [Ti-âmat] with thy holy incantation.
Ride on the storm [chari]ot with all speed!
. . . . !"
The lord rejoiced at the word of his father;
His heart exulted, and he said to his father:
"Creator of the gods, destiny of the great gods,
If I am to be your champion,
To vanquish Ti'âmat, and to keep you alive,
Summon a meeting, make my lot unsurpassable (and) proclaim (it).
When ye are joyfully seated together in the Assembly Hall,
May I through the utterance of my mouth determine the destinies,
    instead of you,
Whatever I create shall remain unaltered,
The command of my lips shall not return (void), it shall not be
    changed."

Anshar sends his vizier Gaga to an older generation of gods, Lahha and Lahâmu. Gaga repeats all that has transpired and bids the gods to attend an assembly to bestow power upon Marduk.

When Lahha and Lahâmu heard (this) they cried aloud,
All the Igigi cried painfully:
"What has happened that she has come to [such a de]cision?
We do not understand Ti'âmat's ac[tion]!"
They gathered themselves together and departed,
All the great gods, who determine the destinies.
They entered into the presence of Anshar and filled [the Assembly
    Hall];
They kissed one another in the assembly;
They set (their) tongues (in readiness) [and sat down] to the banquet;
They ate bread (and) drank(?) [wine].
The sweet drink dispelled their fears;
(So that) they sang for joy as they drank the strong drink.
Exceedingly carefree were they, their heart was exalted;
For Marduk, their champion, they decreed the destiny.
They erected for him a lordly throne, and
He took his place before his fathers for the consultation.
"Thou art (the most) honored among the great gods,
Thy destiny is beyond compare, thy command is (like) Anu('s).
O Marduk, thou art (the most) honored among the great gods,
Thy destiny is beyond compare, thy command is (like) Anu('s).
From this day onward thy command shall not be changed.
To exalt and to abase—this (power) shall be (in) thy hand!

Established shall be the word of thy mouth, incontestable thy
    command!
No one among the gods shall encroach upon thy prerogative.
Maintenance is the requirement of the sanctuaries of the gods;
(And so) the place of their shrines shall be established in thy place.
Thou, O Marduk, art our champion;
To thee we have given kingship over the whole universe.
(Therefore) when thou sittest in the assembly, exalted shall be thy
    word.
May thy weapons not miss, may they smite thy foes.
O lord, preserve the life of him who puts his trust in thee;
But as for the god who started (this) trouble, pour out his life."
Then they placed a garment in their midst;
To Marduk, their first-born, they said:
"Verily, O lord, thy destiny is supreme among the gods,
Command 'to destroy and to create,' (and) it shall be!
By the word of thy mouth let the garment be destroyed;
Command again, and let the garment be whole!"
He commanded with his mouth, and the garment was destroyed.
Again he commanded, and the garment was restored.
When the gods, his fathers, beheld the efficacy of his word,
They rejoiced (and) did homage, (saying:) "Marduk is king!"
They bestowed upon him the sceptor, the throne, and the *palû*;
They gave him an unrivaled weapon to smite the enemy, (saying:)
"Go and cut off the life of Ti'âmat.
May the winds carry her blood to out-of-the-way places."
After the gods, his fathers, had determined the destinies of Bêl,
They set him on the road—the way to success and attainment.
He made a bow and decreed (it) as his weapon;
An arrow he caused to ride (thereon and) fixed the bow-cord.
He lifted up the club and grasped (it) in his right hand;
The bow and the quiver he hung at his side.
The lightning he set before him;
With a blazing flame he filled his body.
He made a net to inclose Ti'âmat within (it),
And had the four winds take (their positions), that nothing of her
    might escape,
The south wind, the north wind, the east wind, (and) the west wind.
The net, the gift of his (grand) father, Anu, he hung at his side.
He created *imhullu*: the evil wind, the whirlwind, the hurricane,
The fourfold wind, the sevenfold wind, the cyclone, the wind
    incomparable.
He sent forth the winds which he had created, the seven of them;
To trouble Ti'âmat within, they rose behind him.
The lord raised up the flood-storm, his mighty weapon.
He mounted the chariot, the storm incomparable (and) terrible
He harnessed for it a team of four and yoked them to it,
The Destructive, the Pitiless, the Trampler, the Fleet.

Sharp and poisonous were their teeth;

They knew how to destroy, they had learned to trample underfoot;

[. . . .] they smote, they were frightful in battle; . . .

For his clothing he wore a terrifying coat of mail;

With terror-inspiring rays his head was covered.

The lord took a direct route and pursued his way;

Toward the place of raging Ti'âmat he set his face.

He held between [his] lips [a talisman (?)] of red clay;

An herb to destroy the poison he grasped in his hand.

Then they crowded(?) around him, the gods crowded(?) around him;

The gods, his fathers, crowded(?) around him, the gods crowded(?) around him.

The lord approached to look into the heart of Ti'âmat,

(And) to see the plan of Kingu, her spouse.

He looks up and is confused in his plan;

Distracted is his mind and disordered his action.

Likewise the gods, his helpers, who were marching by his side,

When they saw the valiant hero, their vision became blurred.

(But) Ti'âmat cast [her spell] without turning her neck,

Upholding with her lips (her) meanness(?) (and) rebellion, (saying:)

"[. . . .] . . . .

They have (not) assembled from their place to thy place, (have they)?"

Then the lord [raised up] the flood-storm, his mighty weapon;

[Ti]'âmat, who was furious, thus he addressed:

"[. .] . . , thou has exalted thyself on high.

Thy heart has prompted (thee) to stir up conflict.

[. . . .] the sons deal unjustly with their fathers;

(And) thou, their bearer, dost hate . . [. .].

[Thou] hast exalted Kingu to be [thy] spouse;

[A divine power] which does not befit thee thou has set up in place of the divine power of Anu.

Against Anshar, the king of the gods, thou seekest evil;

[Against] the gods, my fathers, thou hast directed thy wickedness.

Let thy forces be drawn up, let thy weapons be girded on!

Then come on and let us, me and thee, do battle!"

When Ti'âmat heard this,

She became like one in a frenzy (and) lost her reason. . . .

To the (very) roots her legs shook back and forth.

She recites an incantation (and) repeatedly casts her spell;

And the gods of battle sharpen their weapons.

Ti'âmat and Marduk, the wisest of the gods, took their stand opposite each other,

They pressed on to the battle, they approached in combat.

The lord spread out his net and enmeshed her,

The evil wind, following after, he let loose in her face.

When Ti'âmat opened her mouth to devour him,

He drove in the evil wind, so that she could not close her lips.

As the raging winds filled her belly,

Her belly was distended, and she opened wide her mouth.
He shot off an arrow, it tore her belly,
It cut through her inward parts, it pierced (her) heart.
When he had subdued her, he destroyed her life;
He cast down her carcass (and) stood upon it.
After he had slain Ti'âmat, the leader,
Her band broke to pieces (and) her host dispersed.
Likewise the gods, her helpers, who marched at her side,
Trembled for fear (and) turned back.
They tried to break away to save their lives,
(But) they were completely surrounded, (so that) it was impossible
    to flee.
He bound them and broke their weapons.
Into the net they were drawn and in the snare they were;
They stood within the inclosed spaces (and) were filled with grief;
They bore his wrath, they were confined in the prison.
Likewise the eleven (kinds of) creatures which she had filled with
    awfulness,
The host of demons that marched [.... be]fore her,
He cast into fetters, their hands [he ....];
With (all) their resistance, [he t]rampled (them) underfoot.
And Kingu, who had become chief among them,
He bound and delivered to Uggae.
He took from him the tablet of destinies, which was not his rightful
    possession.
He sealed (it) with a seal and fastened (it) on his breast.
When he had vanquished (and) subdued his enemies,
Had suppressed the arrogant foe ....,
Had fully established Anshar's victory over the enemy,
Had attained the desire of Nudimmud, the valiant Marduk
Strengthened his hold upon the captive gods
And returned to Ti'âmat, whom he had subdued.
The lord trod upon the legs of Ti'âmat,
And with his unsparing club he split (her) skull.
He cut open the arteries of her blood
And caused the north wind to carry (it) to out-of-the-way places.
When his fathers saw (that), they were glad (and) rejoiced
(And) sent greeting-gifts to him.
The lord rested, to look at her dead body, (to see)
How he might divide the colossus (and) create wondrous things
    (therewith).
He split her open like a mussel(?) into two parts;
Half of her he set in place and formed the sky (therewith).
He fixed the bar (and) posted guards;
He commanded them not to let her water escape.
He crossed the heaven and examined (its) regions.
He placed himself opposite the *Apsû*, the dwelling of Nudimmud.
The lord measured the dimensions of the *Apsû*,

And a great structure, its counterpart, he established, (namely),
    Esharra,
The great structure Esharra which he made as a canopy.
Anu, Enlil, and Ea he (then) caused to establish their residence.

After setting the heavens in order, Marduk orders that one of the perpetrators of the war, Kingu, be brought before him.

Marduk assembled the great gods, ordering (them) kindly and giving
    instruction.
He opened his mouth, charging the gods,
The king, speaking a word to the Anunnaki, (saying:)
"Verily, we declared the truth to you before;
(And now) ye shall tell the truth under an oath (?) by me.
Who was it that created the strife,
And caused Ti'âmat to revolt and prepare for battle?
Let him who created the strife be delivered up;
I will make him bear his punishment, (but) ye shall dwell in peace."
The Igigi, the great gods, answered him,
The "king of the gods of heaven and of earth," the counselor of the
    gods, their lord;
"It was Kingu who created the strife
And caused Ti'âmat to revolt and prepare for battle."
They bound him (and) held him in prison before Ea;
Punishment they inflicted upon him by cutting open (the arteries of)
    his blood.
With his blood they fashioned mankind;
He imposed the service of the gods (upon them) and set the gods
    free.

ENUMA ELISH
Translated by Alexander Heidel

Creation by the thought or word of a higher being is a common cosmological motif. It is found in the following monologue of Ra, the sun-god, from the Egyptian Book of Overthrowing Apopis. *The work dates from the Middle Kingdom (or about 1800 B.C.). The line "Then they brought with them my eye" in an allusion to another myth wherein the eye of the sun-god departs for a foreign land but is brought back by Shu and Tefnut.*

The Lord of All, after having come into being, says: I am he who came into being as Khepri (i.e., the Becoming One). When I came into being, the beings came into being, all the beings came into being after I became. Numerous are those who became, who came out of my mouth, before heaven ever existed, nor earth came into being, nor the worms, nor snakes were created in this place. I, being in weariness, was bound to them in the Watery Abyss. I found no place to stand. I thought in my heart, I planned in myself, I made all forms being alone, before I ejected Shu [the air], before I spat out Tefnut [the moist], before any other who was in me had became. Then I planned in my own heart, and many forms of beings came into being as forms of children, as forms of their children. I conceived by my hand, I united myself with my hand, I poured out of my own mouth. I ejected Shu, I spat out Tefnut. It was my father the Watery Abyss who brought them up, and my eye followed them (?), while they became far from me. After having become one god, there were (now) three gods in me. When I came into being in this land, Shu and Tefnut jubilated in the Watery Abyss in which they were. Then they brought with them my eye. After I had joined together my members, I wept over them, and men came into being out of the tears which came out of my eyes. Then she (the eye) became enraged after she came back and had found that I had placed another in her place, that she had been replaced by the Brilliant One. Then I found a higher place for her on my brow, and when she began to rule over the whole land her fury fell down on the flowering (?) and I replaced what she had ravished. I came out of the flowering (?), I created all snakes, and all that came into being with them. Shu and Tefnut produced Geb and Nut; Geb and Nut produced out of a single body Osiris, Horus the Eyeless One, Seth, Isis, and Nephthys, one after the other among them. Their children are numerous in this land.

BOOK OF OVERTHROWING APOPIS
Translated by Alexandre Piankoff

Hesiod has been called the father of Greek didactic poetry. His Theogony *was composed in the eighth century* B.C. *and is an account of the beginning of the world and the birth of the earliest generation of Greek gods. The first of these were Chaos, Earth, Eros, and Heaven.*

Hail! children of Zeus, and grant delectable song. Sing ye the holy race of the deathless gods which are for ever: even them that were born of Earth, and starry Heaven, and dusky Night, and those whom the briny Sea brought forth. And declare ye how in the beginning Gods and Earth came into being, and Rivers and the infinite Sea with raging flood, and the shining Stars, and the wide Heaven above, and the gods which sprang from them, givers of good things: and how they divided their wealth, and how they apportioned their honours; yea, and how at the first they possessed them of many-folded Olympos. These things even from the beginning declare ye unto me, O Muses who dwell in the halls of Olympos, and tell me which of them was first created.

First verily was created Chaos, and then broad-bosomed Earth, the habitation unshaken for ever of all the deathless gods who keep the top of snowy Olympos, and misty Tartaros within the wide-wayed Earth, and Love (Eros) which is the fairest among the deathless gods: which looseth the limbs and overcometh within the breasts of all gods and all men their mind and counsel wise.

From Chaos sprang Erebos and black Night: and from Night in turn sprang Bright Sky (Ether) and Day whom Night conceived and bare after loving union with Erebos. And Earth first bare the starry Heaven, of equal stature to herself, that he might cover her utterly about, to the end that there might be for the blessed gods an habitation steadfast for ever. And she bare the lofty Hills, the pleasant haunts of the goddess Nymphs which dwell among the gladed Hills. Also she bare the unharvested deep with raging flood, even the Sea (Pontos), without the sweet rites of love. And then in the bed of Heaven (Uranus) she bare the deep-eddying Okeanos, and Koios, and Krios, and Hyperion, and Iapetos, and Theia, and Rhea, and Themis, and Mnemosyne, and Thebe of the golden crown, the lovely Tethys. And after these was born her youngest son, even Kronos of crooked counsels, of all her children most terrible, and he hated his lusty Sire.

And again she bare the Kyklopes of overweening heart—Brontes and Steropes, and stout-hearted Arges; which gave to Zeus thunder and fashioned for him the thunderbolt. Now they in all else were like unto the gods, but one only eye was set in the midst of their forehead. These were mortal sons of immortals, of human speech, and Kyklopes was the name whereby they were called, because one round eye was set in their forehead: strength and violence and craft were in their works.

And again there were born of Earth and Heaven three sons mighty and strong beyond naming, Kottos and Briareos and Gyes, children proud. These had a hundred arms shooting from their shoulders, unapproachable, and each fifty heads growing from their shoulders on stout limbs: and unapproachable was the mighty strength which clothed their giant stature. For of all the sons of Earth and Heaven these were the most terrible, and they were hated of their Sire from the beginning; and so soon as any of his sons were born, he would hide them every one in a covert of Earth and allow them not to rise up into light, and he rejoiced in his evil work. But giant Earth was straitened, and groaned within her, and she devised a crafty device. Straightway she created the breed of grey adamant, and fashioned a mighty sickle, and showed the matter unto her dear children, and spake enheartening them, though her own heart was smitten with anguish.

'Sons mine, and of a sinful father, if ye will hearken to me, we would avenge the evil entreatment of your father: for he first devised unseemly deeds.' So she spake: and fear seized them all, and none spake a word. But mighty Kronos of the crooked counsels took heart and answered his good mother, saying: 'Mother, I would undertake and fulfil this deed, since I reck not of our father of evil name: for he first devised unseemly deeds.'

So he spake, and giant Earth rejoiced greatly in her heart, and she set and hid him in an ambush, and put in his hands a sickle of jagged teeth, and put in his heart all manner of guile. Now mighty Heaven came bringing on Night, and yearning for love he laid him about Earth and stretched him all about her. Then from his ambush his son reached forth his left hand, and in his right he took the jagged sickle, long, of jagged teeth, and speedily he shore away his own father's privy parts, and cast them to the winds behind him. And not vainly did they fall from his hands. For all the bloody drops that were sped from his hand did Earth receive, and with the circling seasons she bare the strong Erinyes [Spirits of Vengeance] and the mighty Giants, shining in their armour and holding long spears in their hands, and the Nymphs whom men call the Meliai over the limitless earth. And even as at first he cut off the privy parts with the adamant and hurled them from the mainland into the foaming sea, even so were they borne over the sea for a long time, and from the flesh immortal a white foam arose around it, and therein a maiden grew. And first she came nigh unto holy Kythera, whence next she came to sea-girt Kypros. And she came forth as a reverend goddess beautiful, and around her the grass waxed under her tender feet. Her do gods and men call Aphrodite, the foam-born goddess and fair-crowned Kythereia; for that she was nurtured in foam: and Kythereia because she had chanced upon Kythera: and Kypros-born because she was born in sea-washed Kypros. . . . And with her followed Love (Eros), and fair Desire, both at her birth in the beginning, and when she entered into the company of the gods. And this honour she hath from the beginning, and this fate hath she allotted her among men, and among the deathless gods, even dalliance of maidens, and smiles, and deceits, and sweet delight, and love, and kindliness.

But those children, whom he had himself begotten, mighty Heaven called Titans, naming them reproachfully: for he said that by straining in their folly they had wrought an awful deed, wherefor there should be vengeance afterward.

HESOID'S THEOGONY
Translated by A. W. Mair

The Vedas are Hinduism's oldest extant scriptures and are four in number. First and foremost among them is the Rig Veda. *Dating from approximately 1300 B.C., it contains more than one thousand hymns in praise of various gods. In the following, the act of creation is accomplished by the sacrifice and dismemberment of a primordial giant named Purusa.*

Thousand-headed was Purusa, thousand-eyed, thousand-footed. He having covered the earth on all sides, extended beyond it the length of ten fingers.

Purusa is this all, that has been and that will be. And he is the lord of immortality, which he grows beyond through food.

Such is his greatness, and more than that is Purusa. A fourth of him is all beings, three-fourths of him are what is immortal in heaven.

With three quarters Purusa rose upward; one quarter of him here came into being again. Thence he spread asunder in all directions to what eats and does not eat.

From him Viraj was born, from Viraj Purusa. When born he reached beyond the earth behind and also before.

When the gods performed a sacrifice with Purusa as an oblation, the spring was its melted butter, the summer its fuel, the autumn its oblation.

That Purusa, born in the beginning, they besprinkled as a sacrifice on the strew: with him the gods, the Sadhyas, and the seers sacrificed.

From that sacrifice completely offered was collected the clotted butter: he made that the beasts of the air, of the forest, and those of the village.

From that sacrifice completely offered were born the hymns and the chants; the metres were born from it; the sacrificial formula was born from it.

From that arose horses and all such as have two rows of teeth. Cattle were born from that; from that were born goats and sheep.

When they divided Purusa, into how many parts did they dispose him? What (did) his mouth (become)? What are his two arms, his two thighs, his two feet called?

His mouth was the Brahman, his two arms were made the warrior, his two thighs the Vaisya; from his two feet the Sudra was born.

The moon was born from his mind; from his eye the sun was born; from his mouth Indra and Agni, from his breath Vayu was born.

From his navel was produced the air; from his head the sky was evolved; from his two feet the earth, from his ear the quarters: thus they fashioned the worlds.

Seven were his enclosing sticks; thrice seven were the faggots made, when the gods performing the sacrifice bound Purusa as the victim.

With the sacrifice the gods sacrificed to the sacrifice: these were the first ordinances. These powers reached the firmament where are the ancient Sadhyas, the gods.

RIG VEDA X: 90, 1–16
Translated by Arthur Anthony MacDonell

In contrast to the cosmological myth of Purusa, the Rig Veda *also contains a more speculative hymn wherein the creation of the world is explained as the evolution of the existent from the nonexistent. But, concludes the hymn, "Who knows truly? Who shall here declare, whence it has been produced, whence is this creation?"*

There was not the non-existent nor the existent then; there was not the air nor the heaven which is beyond. What did it contain? Where? In whose protection? Was there water, unfathomable, profound?

There was not death nor immortality then. There was not the beacon of night, nor of day. That one breathed, windless, by its own power. Other than that there was not anything beyond.

Darkness was in the beginning hidden by darkness; indistinguishable, this all was water. That which, coming into being, was covered with void, that One arose through the power of heat.

Desire in the beginning came upon that, (desire) that was the first seed of mind. Sages seeking in their hearts with wisdom found out the bond of the existent in the non-existent.

Their cord was extended across: was there below or was there above? there were impregnators, there were powers; there was energy below, there was impulse above.

Who knows truly? Who shall here declare, whence it has been produced, whence is this creation? By the creation of this (universe) the gods (come) afterwards: who then knows whence it has arisen?

Whence this creation has arisen; whether he founded it or did not: he who is the highest heaven is its surveyor, he only knows, or else he knows not.

RIG VEDA X: 129, 1–7
Translated by Arthur Anthony MacDonell

The Kojiki, *which literally means "Record of Ancient Things," is the oldest extant book in Japanese. Completed in A.D. 712 under the auspices of the imperial court, it is a compilation of Japanese myths, folk etymologies, and genealogies. In the opening chapters, the seven generations of gods come into existence. These include the creator deities Izanagi and Izanami, who give birth not only to thirty-five other gods but also to the islands of Japan.*

At the time of the beginning of heaven and earth, there came into existence in TAKAMA-NO-PARA a deity named AME-NO-NI-NAKA-NUSI-NO-KAMI; next, TAKA-MI-MUSUBI-NO-KAMI; next, TAKA-MI-MUSUBI-NO-KAMI; next, KAMI-MUSUBI-NO-KAMI. These three deities all came into existence as single deities, and their forms were not visible.

Next, when the land was young, resembling floating oil and drift-like a jellyfish, there sprouted forth something like reed-shoots. From these came into existence the deity UMASI-ASI-KABI-PIKO-DI-NO-KAMI; next, AME-NO-TOKO-TATI-NO-KAMI. These two deities also came into existence as single deities, and their forms were not visible.

The five deities in the above section are the Separate Heavenly Deities.

Next there came into existence the deity KUNI-NO-TOKO-TATI-NO-KAMI; next, TOYO-KUMO-NO-NO-KAMI. These two deities also came into existence as single deities, and their forms were not visible.

Next there came into existence the deity named U-PIDI-NI-NO-KAMI; next, his spouse SU-PIDI-NI-NO-KAMI. Next, TUNO-GUPI-NO-KAMI; next, his spouse IKU-GUPI-NO-KAMI. Next, OPO-TO-NO-DI-NO-KAMI; next, his spouse OPO-TO-NO-BE-NO-KAMI. Next, OMO-DARU-NO-KAMI; next, his spouse AYA-KASIKO-NE-NO-KAMI. Next, IZANAGI-NO-KAMI; next, his spouse IZANAMI-NO-KAMI.

The deities in the above section, from KUNI-NO-TOKO-TATI-NO-KAMI through IZANAMI-NO-KAMI, are called collectively the Seven Generations of the Age of the Gods.

At this time the heavenly deities, all with one command, said to the two deities IZANAGI-NO-MIKOTO and IZANAMI-NO-MIKOTO:

"Complete and solidify this drifting land!"

Giving them the Heavenly Jeweled Spear, they entrusted the mission to them.

Thereupon, the two deities stood on the Heavenly Floating Bridge and, lowering the jeweled spear, stirred with it. They stirred the brine with a churning-churning sound; and when they lifted up [the spear] again, the brine dripping down from the tip of the spear piled up and became an island. This was the island ONOGORO.

Descending from the heavens to this island, they erect a heavenly pillar and a spacious palace.

At this time [IZANAGI-NO-MIKOTO] asked his spouse IZANAMI-NO-MIKOTO, saying:

"How is your body formed?"

She replied, saying:

"My body, formed though it be formed, has one place which is formed insufficiently."

Then IZANAGI-NO-MIKOTO said:

"My body, formed though it be formed, has one place which is formed to excess. Therefore, I would like to take that place in my body which is formed to excess and insert it into that place in your body which is formed insufficiently, and [thus] give birth to the land. How would this be?"

IZANAMI-NO-MIKOTO replied, saying:

"That will be good."

Then IZANAGI-NO-MIKOTO said:

"Then let us, you and me, walk in a circle around this heavenly pillar and meet and have conjugal intercourse."

After thus agreeing, [IZANAGI-NO-MIKOTO] then said:

"You walk around from the right, and I will walk around from the left and meet you."

After having agreed to this, they circled around; then IZANAMI-NO-MIKOTO said first:

"*Ana-ni-yasi*, how good a lad!"

Afterwards, IZANAGI-NO-MIKOTO said:

"*Ana-ni-yasi*, how good a maiden!"

After each had finished speaking, [IZANAGI-NO-MIKOTO] said to his spouse:

"It is not proper that the woman speak first."

Nevertheless, they commenced procreation and gave birth to a leech-child. They placed this child into a boat made of reeds and floated it away.

Next, they gave birth to the island of APA. This also is not reckoned as one of their children.

Then the two deities consulted together and said:

"The child which we have just borne is not good. It is best to report [this matter] before the heavenly deities."

Then they ascended together and sought the will of the heavenly deities. The heavenly deities thereupon performed a grand divination and said:

"Because the woman spoke first, [the child] was not good. Descend once more and say it again."

Then they descended again and walked once more in a circle around the heavenly pillar as [they had done] before.

Then IZANAGI-NO-MIKOTO said first:

"*Ana-ni-yasi*, how good a maiden!"

Afterwards, his spouse IZANAMI-NO-MIKOTO said:

"*Ana-ni-yasi*, how good a lad!" ...

After this second, more successful coupling, Izanagi and Izanami give birth to a total of fourteen islands and thirty-four deities. Izanami dies while giving birth to the last of these, a fire-god.

Thus, at last, IZANAMI-NO-KAMI, because she had borne the fire-deity, divinely passed away.

From AME-NO-TORI-PUNE through TOYO-UKE-BIME-NO-KAMI are altogether eight deities.

All of the islands borne by the two deities IZANAGI and IZANAMI were fourteen; the deities [borne by them were] thirty-five.

These were born before IZANAMI-NO-KAMI divinely passed away. However, the island ONOGORO was not born. Also the leech-child and island of APA are not reckoned as their children.

At this time IZANAGI-NO-MIKOTO said:

"Alas, I have given my beloved spouse in exchange for a mere child!"

Then he crawled around her head and around her feet, weeping.

At this time in his tears there came into existence the deity who dwells at the foot of the trees in the foothill of Mount KAGU, named NAKI-SAPA-ME-NO-KAMI.

Then he buried the departed IZANAMI-NO-KAMI on Mount PIBA, the border between the land of IDUMO and the land of PAPAKI.

KOJIKI
Translated by Donald L. Philippi

Norse cosmogony finds its most comprehensive and dramatic expression in the Völuspá, *or "Prophecy of the Seeress," from the* Poetic Edda. *A seeress is summoned from the grave by the sovereign god Othin. Her tale begins with a vision of the abyss, when "neither earth was there nor upper heaven, but a gaping nothing and green things nowhere." Creation is effected by the gods, and soon giants, dwarfs, and humans dwell on the earth. An age of innocence ends with the coming of the Norns, or Fates, and the slaying of Gullveig, which precipitates a cosmic war. The original confrontation between the AEsir and the Vanir embroils all the gods in a cataclysmic struggle that shakes the world tree Yggdrasill to its very roots. Baldr, god of light, is slain, and evil and the powers of destruction are unleashed on the world. But the seeress concludes her apocalyptic vision with a promise of rebirth; she foresees the creation of a new and better world where Baldr and other benign gods will rule in peace and justice. The Völuspá is profoundly Scandinavian; it dates from the tenth century and is probably the finest epic of the expiring Viking Age.*

1. Hear me, all ye   hallowed beings,
   both high and low   of Heimdall's children:
   thou wilt, Valfather,   that I well set forth
   the foremost fates   which befall the world.

2. I call to mind   the kin of etins
   which in times long gone   did give me life.
   Nine worlds I know,   of nine abodes
   of the wondrous world-tree,   the welkin beneath.

3. In earliest times   did Ymir live:
   was nor sea nor sand   nor salty waves,
   neither earth was there   nor upper heaven,
   but a gaping nothing   and green things nowhere.

4. Was the land then lifted   aloft by Bur's sons
   who made Mithgarth,   the matchless earth;
   shone from the south   the sun on dry land
   on the ground then grew   the greensward soft.

5. From the south the sun,   by the side of the moon,
   heaved his right hand   over heaven's rim;
   the sun knew not   what seat he had,
   the moon knew not   what might he had,
   the stars knew not   what stead they held.

6. Then gathered together   the gods for counsel,
   the holy hosts,   and held converse;
   to night and new-moon   their names they gave,
   the morning named,   and midday also,
   forenoon and evening   to order the year.

7. On Itha-field met   the mighty gods;
   shrines and temples   they timbered high,

forges they formed   to fashion gold,
tongs they did shape   and tools they made;

8. Played at draughts in the garth: right glad they were,
nor aught lacked they   of lustrous gold;—
till maidens three   from the thurses came,
awful in might,   from etin-home.

9. To the coast then came,   kind and mighty,
three great aesir   from that meeting;
on the land they found,   of little strength,
Ask and Embla,   unfated yet.

10. Sense they possessed not,   soul they had not,
being nor bearing   nor blooming hue;
soul gave Othin,   sense gave Hoenir,
being, Lothur,   and blooming hue.

11. An ash I know,   hight Yggdrasil,
the mighty tree   moist with white dews;
thence come the floods   that fall a-down;
evergreen stands   at Urth's well this tree.

12. Thence wise maidens   three betake them—
under spreading boughs   their bower stands—;
[Urth one is hight,   the other, Verthandi,
Skuld the third: they scores did cut,]
they laws did make   they lives did choose:
for the children of men   they marked the fates.

13. I ween the first war   in the world was this,
when the gods Gullveig   gashed with their spears,
and in the hall   of Hor burned her—
three times burned they   the thrice re-born,
ever and anon: even now she liveth.

14. Heith she was hight   where to houses she came,
the wise seeress,   and witchcraft plied—
cast spells where she could,   cast spells on the mind:
to wicked women   she was welcome ever.

15. Then gathered together   the gods for counsel,
the holy hosts,   and held converse:
should the AEsir a truce   with tribute buy,
or should all gods   share in the feast.

16. His spear did Othin   speed o'er the host:
the first of feuds   was thus fought in the world;

was broken in battle   the breastwork of Asgarth,
fighting Vanir   the field trampled.

17. Then gathered together   the gods for counsel,
the holy hosts,   and held converse:
who had filled the air   with foul treason,
and to uncouth etins   Oth's wife given.

18. Thewy Thor then   overthrew the foe,—
he seldom sits   when of such he hears:
were sworn oaths broken   and solemn vows,
gods' plighted troth,   the pledges given.

19. Where Heimdall's horn   is hid, she knows,
under heaven-touching   holy world-tree;
on it are shed   showery falls
from Fiolnir's pledge: know ye further, or how?

20. Alone she sat out   when the lord of gods,
Othin the old,   her eye did seek:
"what seekest to know,   why summon me?
Well know I, Ygg,   where thy eye is hidden."

21. She knows that Othin's   eye is hidden
in the wondrous   well of Mimir;
each morn Mimir   his mead doth drink
out of Fiolnir's pledge: know ye further, or how?

22. Gave Ygg to her   armrings and gems
for her seeress' sight   and soothsaying:
(the fates I fathom,   yet farther I see,)
see far and wide   the worlds about.

23. The valkyries' flock   from afar she beholds,
ready to ride   to the realm of men:
Skuld held her shield,   Skogul likewise,
Guth, Hild, Gondul,   and Geirskogul:
[for thus are hight   Herian's maidens,
ready to ride   o'er reddened battlefields].

24. I saw for Baldr,   the blessed god,
Ygg's dearest son   what doom is hidden:
green and glossy,   there grew aloft,
the trees among,   the mistletoe.

25. The slender-seeming   sapling became
a fell weapon   when flung by Hoth;
but Baldr's brother   was born full soon:

but one night old   slew him Othin's son.

26. Neither cleansed his hands   nor combed his hair
     till Baldr's slayer   he sent to Hel;
     but Frigg did weep   in Fensalir
     the fateful deed: know ye further, or how?

27. A captive lies   in the kettle-grove,
     like to lawless   Loki in shape;
     there sits Sigyn,   full sad in mind,
     by her fettered mate: know ye further, or how?

28. There flows from the east,   through festerdales,
     a stream hight Slith,   filled with swords and knives.

29. Waist-deep wade there   through waters swift
     mainsworn men   and murderous,
     eke those who betrayed   a trusted friend's wife;
     there gnas Nithhogg   naked corpses,
     there the Wolf rends men   —wit ye more, or how?

30. Stood in the north   on the Nitha-fields
     a dwelling golden   which the dwarves did own;
     an other stood   on Okolnir,
     that etin's beer-hall   who is Brimir hight.

31. A hall standeth   from the sun so far,
     on Na-strand's shore: turn north its doors;
     drops of poison   drip through the louver,
     its walls are clad   with coiling snakes.

32. In the east sat the old one,   in the Ironwood,
     bred there the bad   brood of Fenrir;
     will one of these,   worse than they all,
     the sun swallow   in seeming a wolf.

33. He feeds on the flesh   of fallen men,
     with their blood sullies   the seats of the gods;
     will grow swart the sunshine   in summers thereafter,
     the weather woe-bringing: do ye wit more, or how?

34. His harp striking,   on hill there sat
     gladsome Eggther,   he who guards the ogress;
     o'er him gaily   in the gallows-tree
     crowed the fair-red cock   which is Fialar hight.

35. Crowed o'er the gods   Gullinkambi,
     wakes he the heroes   with Herian who dwell;

another crows   the earth beneath
in the halls of Hel,   of hue dark red.

36. Garm bays loudly   before Gnipa cave,
    tears him free Fenrir   and fares to battle.
    The fates I fathom   yet farther I see:
    of the mighty gods   the engulfing doom.

37. Brothers will battle   to bloody end,
    and sisters' sons   their sib betray;
    woe's in the world,   much wantonness;
    [axe-age, sword-age—   sundered are shields—
    wind-age, wolf-age,   ere the world crumbles;]
    will the spear of no man   spare his brother.

38. Mimir's sons dance;   the doom doth break
    when blares the gleaming   old Giallar-horn;
    loud blows Heimdall,   the horn is aloft,
    in Hel's dark hall   horror spreadeth.

39. Trembles the towering   tree Yggdrasil,
    its leaves sough loudly: unleashed is the etin;
    once more Othin   with Mim's head speaketh
    ere the sib of Surt   doth swallow him.

40. What ails the aesir   and what the alfs?
    In uproar all etins—   are the aesir met.
    At the gates of their grots   the wise dwarfs groan
    In their fell-fastnesses: wit ye further, or how?

41. Garm bays loudly   before Gnipa cave,
    tears him free Fenrir   and fares to battle!
    The fates I fathom,   yet farther I see:
    of the mighty gods   the engulfing doom.

42. Fares Hrym from the east,   holding his shield;
    the Mithgarth-worm   in mighty rage
    scatters the waves;   screams the eagle,
    his nib tears the dead;   Naglfar loosens.

43. Sails a ship from the north   with shades from Hel;
    o'er the ocean-stream   steers it Loki;
    in the wake of the Wolf   rush witless hordes
    who with baleful Byleist's   brother do fare.

44. Comes Surt from the south   with the singer-of-twigs,
    the war-god's sword   like a sun doth shine;
    the tall hills totter,   and trolls stagger,

men fare to Hel,   the heavens rive.

45. Another woe   awaiteth Hlin,
    when forth goes Othin   to fight the Wolf,
    and the slayer of Beli   to battle with Surt:
    then Frigg's husband   will fall lifeless.

46. Strides forth Vithar,   Val-father's son,
    the fearless fighter,   Fenrir to slay;
    to the heart he hews   the Hvethrung's son;
    avenged is then   Vithar's father.

47. Comes Hlothyn's son,   the hammer-wielder;
    gapes the grisly   earth-girdling Serpent
    when strides forth Thor   to stay the Worm.

48. Mightily mauls   Mithgarth's warder—
    shall all wights in the world   wander from home—;
    back falls nine steps   Fiorgyn's offspring—
    nor fears for his fame—   from the frightful worm.

49. 'Neath sea the land sinketh,   the sun dimmeth,
    from the heavens fall   the fair bright stars;
    gushes forth steam   and gutting fire,
    to very heaven   soar the hurtling flames.

50. Garm bays loudly   before Gnipa cave,
    tears him free Fenrir   and fares to battle.
    The fates I fathom,   yet farther I see:
    of the mighty gods   the engulfing doom.

51. Again see I,   bright green afresh,
    the earth arise   from out of the sea;
    fell-torrents flow,   overflies them the eagle,
    on hoar highlands   hunting for fish.

52. Again the aesir   on Itha-field meet,
    and speak of the mighty   Mithgarth-worm,—
    go over again   the great world-doom,
    and Fimbultyr's   unfathomed runes.

53. Then in the grass   the golden tablets,
    the far-famed ones   will be found again,
    which they had owned   in olden days,
    (the foremost gods   and Fiolnir's kin).

54. On onsown acres   the ears will grow,
    all bale will be bettered;   will Baldr come then.

Both he and Hoth   with Hropt will dwell
and the war-gods alway: do ye wit more, or how?

55. Will high-souled Hoenir   handle the blood-wands,
and Ygg's brother's sons   forever will dwell
in wide Wind-home: do ye wit more, or how?

56. I see a hall   than the sun more fair,
thatched with red gold,   on Gimle's heights
There will the gods   all guiltless throne,
and live forever   in ease and bliss.

57. A-down cometh   to the doom of the world
the great godhead   which governs all.

58. Comes the darksome   dragon flying,
glossy Nithhogg,   from the Nitha-fells;
he bears in his pinions   as the plains he o'erflies,
naked corpses: now he will sink.

THE POETIC EDDA
Translated by Lee M. Hollander

The Kalevala, *the Finnish national epic, was not compiled until the nineteenth century, although it probably existed in oral form in the Middle Ages. These verses, collected by Elias Lönnrot from folk sources, begin with a creation myth. Later runes detail the adventures of three semidivine brothers—Wainamoinen, Ilmarinen, and Lemminkainen—who dwell in mythical Kalevala, the land of heroes. The eight-syllable trochaic line and epic form of the* Kalevala *was imitated by Longfellow in* Hiawatha.

In primeval times, a maiden,
Beauteous Daughter of the Ether,
Passed for ages her existence
In the great expanse of heaven,
O'er the prairies yet enfolded.
Wearisome the maiden growing,
Her existence sad and hopeless,
Thus alone to live for ages
In the infinite expanses
Of the air above the sea-foam,
In the far outstretching spaces,
In a solitude of ether,
She descended to the ocean,
Waves her couch, and waves her
    pillow.
Thereupon the rising storm-wind
Flying from the East in fierceness,

Whips the ocean into surges,
Strikes the stars with sprays of
    ocean
Till the waves are white with
    fervor.
To and fro they toss the maiden,
Storm-encircled, hapless maiden;
With her sport the rolling
    billows,
With her play the storm-wind
    forces,
On the blue back of the waters;
On the white-wreathed waves of
    ocean,
Play the forces of the salt-sea,
With the lone and helpless
    maiden;

Till at last in full conception,
Union now of force and beauty,
Sink the storm-winds into
   slumber;
Overburdened now the maiden
Cannot rise above the surface;
Seven hundred years she
   wandered,
Ages nine of man's existence,
Swam the ocean hither, thither,
Could not rise above the waters,
Conscious only of her travail;
Seven hundred years she labored
Ere her first-born was delivered.
Thus she swam as water-mother,
Toward the east, and also
   southward,
Toward the west, and also
   northward;
Swam the sea in all directions,
Frightened at the strife of
   storm-winds,
Swam in travail, swam unceasing,
Ere her first-born was delivered.

Then began she gently weeping,
Spake these measures,
   heavy-hearted:
"Woe is me, my life hard-fated!
Woe is me, in this my travail!
Into what have I now fallen?
Woe is me, that I unhappy,
Left my home in subtle ether,
Came to dwell amid the
   sea-foam,
To be tossed by rolling billows,
To be rocked by winds and
   waters,
On the far outstretching waters,
In the salt-sea's vast expanses,
Knowing only pain and trouble!
Better far for me, O Ukko!
Were I maiden in the Ether,
Than within these ocean-spaces,
To become a water-mother!
All this life is cold and dreary,
Painful here is every motion,
As I linger in the waters,

As I wander through the ocean.
Ukko, thou O God, up yonder,
Thou the ruler of the heavens,
Come thou hither, thou art
   needed,
Come thou hither, I implore thee,
To deliver me from trouble,
To deliver me in travail.
Come I pray thee, hither hasten,
Hasten more that thou art
   needed,
Haste and help this helpless
   maiden!"

When she ceased her
   supplications,
Scarce a moment onward passes,
Ere a beauteous duck descending,
Hastens toward the
   water-mother,
Comes a-flying hither, thither,
Seeks herself a place for nesting.
Flies she eastward, flies she
   westward.
Circles northward, circles
   southward,
Cannot find a grassy hillock,
Not the smallest bit of verdure;
Cannot find a spot protected,
Cannot find a place befitting,
Where to make her nest in
   safety.
Flying slowly, looking round
   her,
She descries no place for
   resting,
Thinking loud and long debating,
And her words are such as follow
"Build I in the winds my
   dwelling,
On the floods my place of
   nesting?
Surely would the winds destroy
   it,
Far away the waves would wash
   it."

Then the daughter of the Ether,

Now the hapless water-mother,
Raised her shoulders out of
water,
Raised her knees above the ocean,
That the duck might build her
dwelling,
Build her nesting-place in safety.
Thereupon the duck in beauty,
Flying slowly, looking round
her,
Spies the shoulders of the maiden,
Sees the knees of Ether's
daughter,
Now the hapless water-mother,
Thinks them to be grassy
hillocks,
On the blue back of the ocean.
Thence she flies and hovers
slowly,
Lightly on the knee she settles,
Finds a nesting-place befitting,
Where to lay her eggs in safety.
Here she builds her humble
dwelling,
Lays her eggs within, at pleasure,
Six, the golden eggs she lays
there,
Then a seventh, an egg of iron;
Sits upon her eggs to hatch them,
Quickly warms them on the
knee-cap
Of the hapless water-mother;
Hatches one day, then a second,
Then a third day sits and hatches.
Warmer grows the water round
her,
Warmer is her bed in ocean,
While her knee with fire is
kindled,
And her shoulders too are
burning,
Fire in every vein is coursing.
Quick the maiden moves her
shoulders,
Shakes her members in
succession,
Shakes the nest from its
foundation,

And the eggs fall into ocean,
Dash in pieces on the bottom
Of the deep and boundless
waters.
In the sand they do not perish,
Not the pieces in the ocean;
But transformed, in wondrous
beauty
All the fragments come together
Forming pieces two in number,
One the upper, one the lower,
Equal to the one, the other.
From one half the egg, the
lower,
Grows the nether vault of Terra:
From the upper half remaining,
Grows the upper vault of
Heaven;
From the white part comes the
moonbeams,
From the yellow part the
sunshine,
From the motley part the
starlight,
From the dark part grows the
cloudage;
And the days speed onward
swiftly,
Quickly do the years fly over,
From the shining of the new sun
From the lighting of the full
moon.
Still the daughter of the Ether,
Swims the sea as water-mother,
With the floods outstretched
before her,
And behind her sky and ocean.
Finally about the ninth year,
In the summer of the tenth year,
Lifts her head above the surface,
Lifts her forehead from the
waters,
And begins at last her workings.
Now commences her creations,
On the azure water-ridges,
On the mighty waste before her.
Where her hand she turned in
water,

There arose a fertile hillock;
Wheresoe'er her foot she rested,
There she made a hole for fishes;
Where she dived beneath the
    waters,
Fell the many deeps of ocean;
Where upon her side she turned
    her,
There the level banks have risen;
Where her head was pointed
    landward,
There appeared wide bays and
    inlets;
When from shore she swam a
    distance,
And upon her back she rested,
There the rocks she made and
    fashioned,
And the hidden reefs created
Where the ships are wrecked so
    often,
Where so many lives have
    perished.

Thus created were the islands,
Rocks were fastened in the
    ocean,
Pillars of the sky were planted,
Fields and forests were created,
Checkered stones of many
    colors,
Gleaming in the silver sunlight,
All the rocks stood well
    established;
But the singer, Wainamoinen,
Had not yet beheld the sunshine,
Had not seen the golden
    moonlight,
Still remaining undelivered.
Wainamoinen, old and trusty,
Lingering within his dungeon
Thirty summers altogether,
And of winters, also thirty,
Peaceful on the waste of waters,
On the broad-sea's yielding
    bosom,
Well reflected, long considered,
How unborn to live and flourish

In the spaces wrapped in
    darkness,
In uncomfortable limits,
Where he had not seen the
    moonlight,
Had not seen the silver sunshine.
Thereupon these words he
    uttered,
Let himself be heard in this wise:
"Take, O Moon, I pray thee, take
    me,
Take me, thou, O Sun above me,
Take me, thou, O Bear of heaven,
From this dark and dreary
    prison,
From these unbefitting portals,
From this narrow place of
    resting,
From this dark and gloomy
    dwelling,
Hence to wander from the
    ocean,
Hence to walk upon the islands,
On the dry land walk and
    wander,
Like an ancient hero wander,
Walk in open air and breathe it,
Thus to see the moon at evening,
Thus to see the silver sunlight,
Thus to see the Bear in heaven,
That the stars I may consider."

Since the Moon refused to free
    him,
And the sun would not deliver,
Nor the Great Bear give
    assistance,
His existence growing weary,
And his life but an annoyance,
Bursts he then the outer portals
Of his dark and dismal fortress;
With his strong, but unnamed
    finger.
Opens he the lock resisting;
With the toes upon his left foot,
With the fingers of his right
    hand,
Creeps he through the yielding

portals
To the threshold of his dwelling;
On his knees across the
  threshold,
Throws himself head foremost,
  forward
Plunges into deeps of ocean,
Plunges hither, plunges thither,
Turning with his hands the
  water;
Swims he northward, swims he
  southward,
Swims he eastward, swims he
  westward,
Studying his new surroundings.

Thus our hero reached the water,
Rested five years in the ocean,
Six long years, and even seven
  years,
Till the autumn of the eighth

year,
When at last he leaves the
  waters,
Stops upon a promontory,
On a coast bereft of verdure;
On his knees he leaves the ocean,
On the land he plants his right
  foot,
On the solid ground his left foot,
Quickly turns his hands about
  him,
Stands erect to see the sunshine,
Stands to see the golden
  moonlight,
That he may behold the Great
  Bear,
That he may the stars consider.
Thus our hero, Wainamoinen,
Thus the wonderful enchanter
Was delivered from his mother,
Imatar, the Ether's daughter.

THE KALEVALA
Translated by John Martin Crawford

The Popol Vuh, *the sacred book of the ancient Quiché Maya, was transcribed in the Latin alphabet in the mid-sixteenth century by an anonymous but highly educated member of that tribe. This important document contains an account of the cosmogony, mythology, traditions, and history of the Quiché, who were the Guatemala highland's most powerful nation before the Conquest. Its language, style, and philosophy reveal the high degree of learning the Quiché had attained.*

This is the account of how all was in suspense, all calm, in silence; all motionless, still, and the expanse of the sky was empty.

This is the first account, the first narrative. There was neither man, nor animal, birds, fishes, crabs, trees, stones, caves, ravines, grasses, nor forests; there was only the sky.

The surface of the earth had not appeared. There was only the calm sea and the great expanse of the sky.

There was nothing brought together, nothing which could make a noise, nor anything which might move, or tremble, or could make noise in the sky.

There was nothing standing; only the calm water, the placid sea, alone and tranquil. Nothing existed.

There was only immobility and silence in the darkness, in the night. Only the Creator, the Maker, Tepeu, Gucumatz, the Forefathers, were in the water surrounded with light. They were hidden under green and blue feathers, and were therefore called Gucumatz. By nature they were great sages and great thinkers. In this manner the sky existed and also the Heart of Heaven, which is the name of God and thus He is called.

Then came the word. Tepeu and Gucumatz came together in the darkness, in the night, and Tepeu and Gucumatz talked together. They talked then, discussing and deliberating; they agreed, they united their words and their thoughts.

Then while they meditated, it became clear to them that when dawn would break, man must appear. Then they planned the creation, and the growth of the trees and the thickets and the birth of life and the creation of man. Thus it was arranged in the darkness and in the night by the Heart of Heaven who is called Huracán.

The first is called Caculhá Huracán. The second is Chipi-Caculhá. The third is Raxa-Caculhá. And these three are the Heart of Heaven.

Then Tepeu and Gucumatz came together; then they conferred about life and light, what they would do so that there would be light and dawn, who it would be who would provide food and sustenance.

Thus let it be done! Let the emptiness be filled! Let the water recede and make a void, let the earth appear and become solid; let it be done. Thus they spoke. Let there be light, let there be dawn in the sky and on the earth! There shall be neither glory nor grandeur in our creation and formation until the human being is made, man is formed. So they spoke.

Then the earth was created by them. So it was, in truth, that they created the earth. Earth! they said, and instantly it was made.

Like the mist, like a cloud, and like a cloud of dust was the creation, when the mountains appeared from the water; and instantly the mountains grew.

Only by a miracle, only by magic art were the mountains and valleys formed; and instantly the groves of cypresses and pines put forth shoots together on the surface of the earth.

And thus Gucumatz was filled with joy, and exclaimed: "Your coming has been fruitful, Heart of Heaven; and you, Huracán, and you, Chipi-Calculhá, Raxa-Caculhá!"

"Our work, our creation shall be finished," they answered.

First the earth was formed, the mountains and the valleys; the currents of water were divided, the rivulets were running freely between the hills, and the water was separated when the high mountains appeared.

Thus was the earth created, when it was formed by the Heart of Heaven, the Heart of Earth, as they are called who first made it fruitful, when the sky was in suspense, and the earth was submerged in the water.

So it was that they made perfect the work, when they did it after thinking and meditating upon it.

Popol Vuh
Translated by Delia Goetz and Sylvanus G. Morley

Selected Bibliography

Bulfinch, Thomas. *Mythology*. New York: Random House Modern Library, 1937.

Campbell, Joseph. *The Hero with a Thousand Faces*. New York: The Bollingen Foundation, 1949.

———. *The Mythic Image*. New York: The Bollingen Foundation, 1975.

———. *Myths to Live By*. New York: Viking Press, 1972.

Colum, Padraic. *Myths of the World*. New York: Grosset & Dunlap, 1972.

Eliade, Mircea. *Myth and Reality*. New York: Harper & Row, 1963.

Frazer, Sir James. *The Golden Bough*. (12 volumes) London: Macmillan, 1907–15.

Gaster, Theodor. *The Oldest Stories in the World*. New York: Viking Press, 1952.

Graves, Robert. *The Greek Myths*. (2 volumes) Baltimore: Penguin Books, 1955.

Hooke, Samuel H. *Middle Eastern Mythology*. Middlesex, England: Penguin Books, 1963.

Jung, Carl C. *Memories, Dreams, Reflections*. New York: Random House, 1961.

Jung, Carl C. et al. *Man and His Symbols*. New York: Doubleday, 1964.

Kramer, Samuel N. *Mythologies of the Ancient World*. New York: Doubleday, 1961.

Leeming, David A. *Mythology: The Voyage of the Hero*. Philadelphia: J. B. Lippincott, 1973.

Murray, Henry, ed. *Myth and Mythmaking*. Boston: Beacon Press, 1968.

Routh, H.V. *God, Man, and Epic Poetry*. (2 volumes) Cambridge: Cambridge University Press, 1927.

Thompson, William. *At the Edge of History*. New York: Harper & Row, 1972.

Teilhard de Chardin, Pierre. *The Phenomenon of Man*. New York: Harper & Row, 1959.

Watts, Alan. *Myth and Ritual in Christianity*. Boston: Beacon Press, 1968.

Picture Credits

The Editors would like to thank Barbara Nagelsmith in Paris, Russell Ash in London, and Lynn Seiffer in New York for their invaluable assistance.

The following abbreviations are used:

AAM	—Asian Art Museum of San Francisco, Avery Brundage Collection
BM	—British Museum
(G)	—(Giraudon)
(MH)	—(Michael Holford)
L	—Louvre
MMA	—Metropolitan Museum of Art
PM	—Pierpont Morgan Library
MNAM	—Museo Nacional de Antropología, Mexico City
MAI	—Museum of the American Indian, Heye Foundation
(S)	—(Scala)

HALF TITLE Symbol designed by Jay J. Smith Studio. FRONTISPIECE Miniature of Vishnu, Bundi, 1770. Victoria and Albert Museum (S)

CHAPTER 1 **6** Venus, Catal Huyuk, 6th millennium. Ankara Museum (MH) **8** top, Cyprus Museum (Boudot-Lamotte); bottom, Lakhnau Museum (Boudot-Lamotte) **9** top, L(Boudot-Lamotte); bottom, Museum of Primitive Art (Charles Uht) **10** top, Akkadian seal, *ca.* 2300 B.C. BM(MH); bottom, Relief of Gilgamesh, Khorsabad, 8th century B.C. L(G) **11** Stele of King Zet, 1st Dynasty. L(G) **14** top, Statue of Isis, Horus, and Osiris. Brooklyn Museum; bottom, Porta di San Ranieri. Pisa Cathedral (S) **15** Relief of Vishnu and his consorts, Bihar, 12th century. AAM **16** top, Bronze of Shiva and Parvati, Bengal, 9th century. Cleveland Museum of Art, John L. Severance Fund. **16** bottom, Statue of Krishna, Nepal, 18th century. Prince of Wales Museum, Bombay (S) **17** Wallhanging of battle from the *Mahabharata*, Chamba, 18th century. Victoria and Albert Museum.

THE KINGDOM OF THE DEAD 1 **19** Painting from Thebes, 800 B.C. L **20** Statue of Horus, Heliopolis, 30th Dynasty. MMA, Rogers Fund, 1934. **20–21** Papyrus detail from *Book of the Dead of Ani*, 19th Dynasty. BM(MH) **21** top, Pectoral, 19th Dynasty. L(G) **21** bottom, Statue of Chephren, 4th Dynasty. Egyptian Museum, Cairo. **22–23** Papyrus of the Egyptian cosmology. Egyptian Museum, Cairo (John Ross) **22** Francis & Shaw, Inc. **24** top, Papyrus of Shu. BM(MH) **24** center, Papyrus of Tefnut. BM(MH) **24** bottom, Relief of Geb, Tomb of Seti I, Luxor. (Borromeo) **25** Statue of Hathor, Deir el-Bahari, 18th Dynasty. Egyptian Museum, Cairo (Borromeo) **26** top, Statue of Neith, 26th Dynasty. MMA, Rogers Fund, 1944. **26** left, Painting of Hapi, Tomb of Nefertari. (Borromeo) **26** right, Faience of Hapi. BM(MH) **27** Apis Bull, Memphis, 30th Dynasty. BM (MH) **28** top left, Statue of Horus, 19th Dynasty. L(G); top right, Statue of Ptah. Museum of Antiquities, Turin; bottom, Statue of Sekhmet, Karnak. MMA, Gift of Henry Walters, 1915. **29** left, Statuette of Amon, 25th Dynasty. Brooklyn Museum, Charles Edwin Wilbour Fund; top, Museum of African Art, Eliot Elisofon; bottom, Temple of Amon, Karnak (Rosicrucian Order) **30–31** Papyrus detail from *The Book of the Dead of Ani*, 19th Dynasty. BM **32** left, Bronze cat, Early Ptolemaic. MMA, Purchase, 1958; right, Relief of Horus from Pyramid of Se'n-Wosret I, 20th century B.C. MMA, Rogers Fund, 1907–34. **33** top, Statue of Thoth, 22–26th Dynasty. MMA, Chapman Fund, 1958; center, Receptacle for a mummified snake. Brooklyn Museum; bottom, Limestone ram's head, Early Ptolemaic. MMA, Edward S. Harkness, 1917.

CHAPTER 2 **34** Sumerian goat, Ur. BM(MH) **36** Babylonian stele, 7th century B.C. L(G) **37** top, Phoenician ivory, Nimrud. BM (MH); bottom, Agora excavations, Athens. **38** Relief of Buddha under the Bo Tree, Gandhara, 2nd century A.D. MMA, Rogers Fund, 1913. **39** left, Carved doors from stave church, Urnes, Norway. Universitetets Oldsaksamling, Oslo; right, Miniature from Psalter of the Virgin, Amiens, 13th century. PM Ms 729, fol. 354 **40** Musée de l'Homme Paris. **41** Indian drawing, 16th century. Bibliothèque Nationale, Paris, Ms. Mexicain. 90, fol 44. **42** Statue of Akhnaton. Egyptian Museum, Cairo. **43** Red-figure painting of Oedipus. Vatican.

THE MIGHTY OLYMPIANS **45** Relief of Zeus and Hera. Museo Nazionale, Palermo (S) **46** Red-figure painting of Iris and Hera. BM(MH) **46–47** Black-figure amphora of Zeus with Leto and the twins. BM(MH) **48** top, Poseidon, Apollo, and Artemis, Parthenon frieze. BM; bottom, Black-figure amphora of Poseidon and giant. MMA, Gift of F. W. Rhinelander, 1898. **49** The Bologna Crater. Museo Civico, Bologna. **50** Red-figure hydra of Hades and Persephone. MMA, Gift of Matilda Bruce, 1907. **51** top, Relief of Hades and Persephone. National Archeological Museum, Calabria (S); left, Red-figure painting of Demeter, Persephone, and Triptolemus. BM(MH); right, Red-figure krater of Persephone rising. MMA, Fletcher Fund, 1928. **52** Red-figure kylix of the judgment of Paris. Staatliche Museen Preussischer (Mulas) **53** top, Marble head of Aphrodite, 4th century B.C. Archaeological Museum, Taranto (S); bottom, Kylix of Aphrodite, Rhodes, 460 B.C. BM(MH) **54** top, Silver tetradrachum, 450 B.C. American Numismatic Society **54** Statue of Athena, 4th century B.C. National Museum, Athens. **54–55** Black figure amphora of the birth of Athena. Museum of Fine Arts, Boston, H. L. Pierce Fund. **56** Red-figure kylix of Hercules and the Triton. Tarquinia Museum (S); top, Black-figure amphora of Heracles and the Stymphalian birds. BM (MH) **57** left. Red-figure amphora of Hercules and Cerberus. L(G); right, Relief of Hercules and the Nemean Lion. Bibliothèque Nationale, Paris. **58** top, Black-figure amphora of Achilles slaying Penthesileia. BM (MH); bottom, Red-figure hydra of Perseus, with head of Medusa. BM (MH) **59** top, Terra-cotta of Bellerophon riding Pegasus. BM (MH); bottom, Red-figure kylix of the deeds of Theseus. BM (MH) **60** Painting of Dionysus by Exekias. 6th century B.C. Staatliche Antikensammlungen und Glyptothek, Munich, Collection Caecilia Moessner. **61** top, Red-figure amphora of Dionysus and followers. Brooklyn Museum, Gift of R. B. Woodward; bottom,

Terra-cotta of Dionysus on a goat. BM(MH); right, Copy of Praxiteles' Hermes and Dionysus, 330 B.C. Temple of Hera (S) **62** Barberini statue of Hera. Museo Pio Clementino, Vatican (S) **63** left, Statue of Minerva. L(Josse); right, Statue of Jupiter. Museo Pio Clementino, Vatican (S) **64** The Ludovici Mars. Museo delle Terme, Rome (S) **65** left, Mosaic of Neptune. L (Bulloz); right, Fresco of Venus and Mars, Pompeii. Nuseo Nazionale, Naples (S); bottom, Janus on Roman coin. BM(MH) **66** Statue of Bacchus. Museo Nazionale, Naples (S) **66–67** Sarcophagus with procession of Bacchus, 2nd century B.C. Walters Art Gallery. **67** Relief of Pan. Museo Nazionale, Naples (S)

CHAPTER 3 **68** Miniature of the story of Noah, Ethiopia. BM(MH) **70** Terra-cotta of Gilgamesh, Khorsabad. L(MH) **71** Woodcut of Noah's Ark, Cologne Bible, 1478. PM **72** & **73** Both: Mosaics from San Marco, Venice (S)

SAGE, SAVIOUR, AND PROPHET **75** Painting of the Sakyamuni Buddha by Chang Sheng-Wen, Sung Dynasty. National Palace Museum, Taiwan. **76** All: Reliefs of scenes from Buddha's life, Gandhara, 3rd century. AAM **77** Bronze Buddha, Nepal, 19th century. Handicraft Museum, New Delhi (Borromeo) **78** The Temptation of Buddha, 5th century. Prince of Wales Museum, Bombay (S) **79** left, Painting of the Four Encounters of Buddha, China, 9th century. Musée Guimet, Paris (Josse); right, Statue of the fasting Buddha, Gandhara, 3rd century. Central Museum, Lahore (Borromeo) **80** top, Relief of a miracle performed by Buddha, Gandhara, 3rd century. Museum, Karachi (S); bottom, Pottery group of the Paranirvana, China, Ming Dynasty. MMA, Fletcher Fund, 1925. **81** Painting of the Paradise of Amitabha Buddha, Tun-Huang, 8th century. BM, Stein Collection **82** top, Detail from a New Testament ivory book cover, Venice, 12th century. Victoria and Albert Museum. **82–87** Six frescos by Giotto di Bondone of scenes from the life of Jesus, 1310. All: Capella Scrovegni Padua (S) **84** bottom, Detail from an ivory diptych, 5th century. Victoria and Albert Museum **87** bottom, Detail from a New Testament ivory book cover, Venice, 12th century. Victoria and Albert Museum. **88–89** Miniatures of scenes from life of Mohammed. Both: University Library, Edinburgh. **89–92** Miniatures from Darir, *Siyari-i-Nabi*, Turkey, 16th century. All: New York Public Library, Spencer Collection. **93** Bibliothèque Nationale, Paris, Ms. Suppl. Turc. 190 fol 36v.

CHAPTER 4 **94** The *Aeneid*, 5th century A.D. Vatican Library, Cod. Vat. Lat. 3225 fol 45v. **96** Painting of the Nativity of Buddha, Tibet, 17th century. Musée Guimet, Paris (Josse) **97** Detail from Giotto's fresco of the Nativity of Christ, 1310. Capella Scrovegni, Padua (S) **98** Psalter of the Virgin, Amiens, 13th century. PM Ms 729, fol 55 **100** Black-figure amphora of Theseus and the Minotaur, 540 B.C. MMA, Joseph Pulitzer Bequest, 1947. **100–01** Miniature of the Holy Grail. Bibliothèque Nationale, Paris, Ms. Fr. 12577 fol 74v. **101** Red-figure krater of Jason and the Golden Fleece, 5th century B.C. MMA, Harris Brisbane Dick Fund, 1934. **103** Psalter of the Virgin, Amiens, 13th century. PM Ms 729 fol 345 **104** top, Statue of Osiris. Museo Romano, Brescia; bottom, Miniature from the Winchester Psalter, 1160. BM, Ms. Cotton Nero c IV fol 39r. **105** Bibliothèque Nationale, Paris.

GODS OF THE NORTH **107** Gallo-Roman stele of Cernunnos, Apollo, and Mercury. Musée de Reims (G) **108** top left, Gallo-Roman relief of Epona. Musée Antiquites Nationales, St. Germain-en-Laye (Lauros-G); top right, Statue of Mercury. Musée Antiquites Nationales, St. Germain-en-Laye (Archives Photographiques) **108** & **109** Detail from and overall of the Gundestrup Cauldron, 1st century B.C. National Museum, Copenhagen **110** Stone from the island of Gotland, 9th century. Swedish Information Service, **111** top, Bronze statue of Thor, Mjolnir, 1000 A.D. National Museum Reykjavik; bottom, Viking grave amulets. National Historical Museum, Stockholm. **112** top, Eagle from the shield, Treasure of Sutton Hoo. BM(MH); bottom, Lion's head from Oseburg Find. Universitetets Oldsaksamling, Oslo. **113** Helmet from the Treasure of Sutton Hoo. BM(MH) **114–15** The Frank's Casket from the Treasure of Sutton Hoo. BM(MH) **115**

Runestone, Veckholm Church, Enkoping, Sweden. Swedish Information Service. **115** bottom left, Carved head, stave church, Hegge, Norway. Universitetes Oldsaksamling, Oslo; bottom right, Doorjams, Hylestad Church, Setesdal, Norway. Universitetets Oldsaksamling, Oslo

CHAPTER 5 **116** Kachina doll, Hopi, Arizona. MAI **119** Tlingit and Kitskan shaman charms and Kwakiutl bear mask. All: MAI **123** Relief of the mourning Odysseus, 5th century B.C. Agora excavations, Athens. **124** Statue of Athena, 5th century B.C. MMA, Harris Brisbane Dick Fund, 1950. **125** Relief of the return of Odysseus, 460 B.C. MMA, Fletcher Fund, 1930.

THE TWO AMERICAS **129** Aztec sun-god, Codex Borgia, Vatican Library, Messicana 1 fol 71. **130** God of fire, Veracruz, 5-8th centuries A.D. MNAM **131** top, Aztec god of creation. MNAM; bottom left, God of maize, Monte Albán. American Museum of Natural History bottom right, Olmec Jaguar, Veracruz. BM **132** left, Aztec rain-god. National Museum, Copenhagen; right, Toltec stele of Quetzalcoatl, 7th century. MNAM **133** Mask of Quetzalcoatl, Teotihuacán, 450–750 A.D. Art Institute of Chicago, Gift of Joseph Antonow, 1962. **134** top, God of death, Veracruz. Museo de Antropología, Jalapa (Groth) **134** bottom, Aztec jaguar, 15th century. MNAM **134–35** Aztec altar of skulls, Tenochtitlán, 15th century. MNAM **135** top, Aztec sacrifice, *Codex Magliabecchiano* Biblioteca Nazionale, Florence; bottom, Mask, Tlatilco, 1100–600 B.C. MNAM **136** top, Mask, Kwakiutl, British Columbia; center, Rattle, Tlingit, Alaska; bottom, Totem pole. All: MAI **137** top, Painted bark, Kwakiutl, Canada; bottom, Wooden beaver, Kwakiutl, British Columbia. All: MAI **138** top, Painted buffalo skin, Dakota Sioux. Musée de l'Homme, Paris. **138–39** From left: Masks from Tuscarora, New York; Seneca, New York; Spiro Mound, Oklahoma; Tlingit, Alaska. All: MAI.

CHAPTER 6 **140** *Apotheosis of Washington.* Henry Francis Dupont Winterthur Museum. **142** Gargoyles. Cathedral de Notre-Dame, Paris (Adam Woolfitt) **143** Guardian Lion. Forbidden City, Peking. **144** Lenin poster. Collection of Russell Ash. **145** *Apotheosis of Lincoln.* Library of Congress. **146** Uncle Sam and John Bull. (Culver Pictures) **147** top, *Puck*, 1900; bottom, Horse armor of Frederick III. **148** Nazi poster, Library of Congress. **152** Miniature of God as Architect of the Universe, Old Testament, France, 13th century. Osterreichische Nationalbibliothek, Vienna, Cod 2554 fol 1v.

IN THE BEGINNING **154–84** Miniatures showing the creation of the world and man, from a 13th-century French Bible. PM Ms. 638.

Index